Historic Pottery of the Pueblo Indians, 1600–1880

HISTORIC POTTERY OF THE PUEBLO INDIANS 1600-1880

By LARRY FRANK

and FRANCIS H. HARLOW

Photographs by Bernard Lopez

New York Graphic Society BOSTON, MASSACHUSETTS

ACKNOWLEDGMENT

The generosity of the following persons and institutions,
who lent the authors Pueblo pottery vessels of the Historic
period for study and photography in the preparation of
the present book, is most gratefully acknowledged: Robert
Ashton, Mr. and Mrs. A. Edgar Benton, Marie Chabot,
John Goodwin, Mr. and Mrs. John Hopkins, Mr. and
Mrs. Dennis Hopper, Mr. and Mrs. Bernard Lopez,
Harvey Mudd, Mr. and Mrs. John Painter, and Betty
Toulouse at the Museum of New Mexico and the School
of American Research, both in Sante Fe, New Mexico,
and Hannah Huse at the University of Colorado Museum,
Boulder, Colorado.

International Standard Book Number 0-8212-0586-2
Library of Congress Catalog Card Number 73-89957

First published 1974 by New York Graphic Society Ltd.
11 Beacon St., Boston, Mass. 02108
First printing 1974

CONTENTS

LIST OF ILLUSTRATIONS

Frontispiece: View of Taos Pueblo

COLOR PLATES

(following pages 32 and 128)

FIGURES

PART ONE
Historic Pottery
of the
Pueblo Indians

PUEBLO INDIAN LANGUAGES
AND PUEBLOS SPEAKING THEM

Keres language family: in Cochiti, Santo Domingo,
  San Felipe, Zia, Santa Ana, Laguna,
    and Acoma pueblos

Tano language family:
  Tewa: in San Juan, Santa Clara, San Ildefonso,
    Pojoaque, Nambe, and Tesuque pueblos along
    the Rio Grande, and Hano, a pueblo in Arizona
  Towa: in Jemez Pueblo and formerly in
    Pecos Pueblo (now extinct)
  Tiwa: in Taos, Picuris, Sandia, and Isleta pueblos

Shoshone language family: in the Hopi pueblos
    of Arizona

Zuni language: in Zuni Pueblo

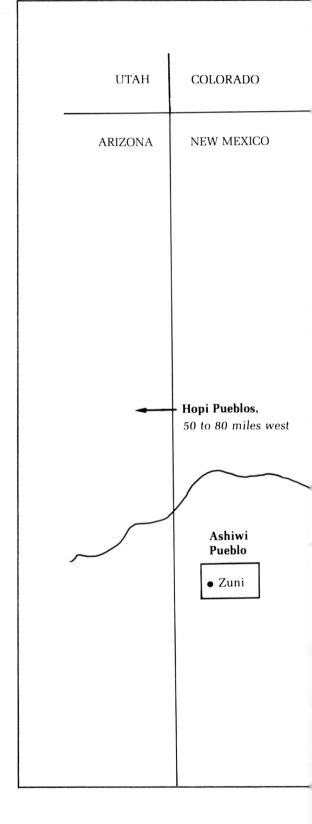

UTAH   COLORADO

ARIZONA   NEW MEXICO

Hopi Pueblos,
50 to 80 miles west

**Ashiwi
Pueblo**

• Zuni

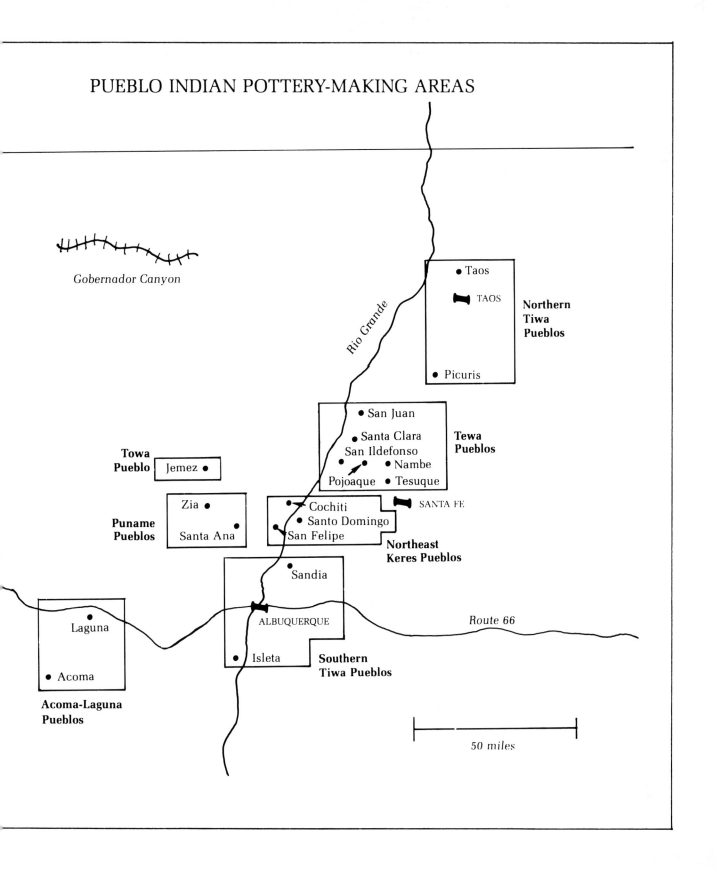

PUEBLO INDIAN POTTERY-MAKING AREAS

Gobernador Canyon

Rio Grande

Taos

TAOS

**Northern
Tiwa
Pueblos**

Picuris

San Juan

Santa Clara

San Ildefonso

Nambe

Pojoaque   Tesuque

**Tewa
Pueblos**

**Towa
Pueblo**   Jemez

Zia

Santa Ana

**Puname
Pueblos**

Cochiti

Santo Domingo

San Felipe

SANTA FE

**Northeast
Keres Pueblos**

Sandia

Laguna

ALBUQUERQUE

Route 66

Acoma

Isleta

**Southern
Tiwa Pueblos**

**Acoma-Laguna
Pueblos**

50 miles

Introduction

The pottery of the Pueblo Indians of the Southwestern United States embodies the highest artistic achievement of a race of quiet, peaceful, and tenacious people who have even to the present day successfully kept their culture intact for over a thousand years. Pottery was to the Pueblo Indians what wood carving was to the Northwest Indians, and bead- and quillwork to Indians of the Plains. The excellence of Pueblo Indian craftsmanship, evidenced in the sculptural form and the decoration of their pottery, rivals that of any European or Oriental Neolithic culture. Pueblo pottery of the Historic period, made from about 1600, when the Spanish arrived in the Southwest, to about 1880, is especially beautiful. After 1880, convenient and safe transportation led to the tourist trade of the modern era, with its generally decadent influence on the serviceability of the pottery. It is with Pueblo pottery of the Historic period, the least known and most handsome of Pueblo ceramics, that this book is principally concerned. Our purpose is to increase the public knowledge and enjoyment of these very considerable treasures.

Historic Pueblo pottery is the least abundantly preserved of all Southwestern pottery and consequently the most difficult to study. Because of the extreme difficulty of importing ceramic wares to the rugged Southwestern frontier, the early Spaniards were forced to use Pueblo pottery to carry out their daily chores. They found it satisfactory for domestic purposes but apparently saw little artistic or esthetic merit in it, hence no collections were made. The collision of the Spaniards and the American Pueblo Indians resulted not only in significant restrictions in the usage of pottery but also in the disappearance of most of that pottery in the first two hundred years of the Historic period. Owing to the orthodoxy of Church authorities, Pueblo Indians were refused the right to bury pottery with their dead in accordance with ancient custom. Instead, they were forced to have Christian burials in cemeteries. Consequently, there are almost no Historic vessels preserved in the relative security of old graves. This was not true of the Prehistoric Indians living before the Europeans made their appearance about 1600. Since this Prehistoric population outnumbered the Historic, it of course made many more vessels. Prehistoric Indians commonly buried their abundant pottery vessels in villages that, now long abandoned, are easy to excavate and to restore for public edification in our day. It was mainly the excavated ancient vessels, shrouded in mystery, that first drew the attention of the public, museums, and scholars to the artistic talents of the Pueblo Indians. In contrast, most pueblos of the Early Historic period are still occupied, and exploration of the old storage or burial sites is generally prohibited.

The significance of the Spanish ban on burial of pottery with the Indian dead cannot be over-emphasized. It is likely that all Prehistoric pottery had some religious aspects, as its burial signifies. But when burial of pottery was prohibited, the Pueblo Indians were forced to concentrate on making pottery exclusively for utilitarian purposes such as storage of grain and water, cooking, etc., while only a small number of vessels were created – in secrecy – for strictly ceremonial use. Ceremonial vessels were carefully guarded and used only on religious occasions closed to outsiders. The heavy brunt of family wear and tear fell upon almost all the rest of the pottery produced. Imagine great-grandmother's set of Dresden, Spode, or Wedgwood in constant use, serving a batallion of families with an endless parade of children! Surely nothing would survive beyond a few cracked and chipped remnants, the rest having long since been discarded. This is what happened to Historic Pueblo pottery; the pottery was used until it was inevitably damaged and broken and then was thrown on the trash heap.

It is regrettable that the few surviving examples of early Historic pottery were so consistently ignored before collectors came on the scene. It was not until about 1880 that James Stevenson and Victor and Cosmos Mindeleff visited Zuni and neighboring pueblos and for the first time brought back to the Smithsonian Institution a typical collection of Historic pottery. No organized effort was made to preserve Historic pottery until the 1920s, when members of the Indian Arts Fund of Santa Fe, as well as a few other imaginative collectors and traders, found that they could still assemble collections. Of the pottery illustrated in this book approximately one-fourth was originally collected by C.G. Wallace; about one-fifth was accumulated by the early enthusiasts of the Indian Arts Fund; nearly one-fourth was accumulated by the Museum of New Mexico; and important reliance has been placed on vessels collected by Earl Morris and J. Gans. To the early enthusiasts we owe most of our knowledge of the field, truly an immense debt. Not until there was sufficient material available for study was there enough interest to inspire the rewarding activity of research on Historic pottery. Only in recent times have accurate methods been developed for dating Historic vessels and identifying the pueblo of origin. These methods are discussed in detail on pages 15–23.

The stage has now been set for an introduction to the imaginative world of a religious and talented people who expressed their spiritual ideas in ceramics and in ceremonies. In the illustrations for this book will be found a cosmology interpreted in rhythm, color, line, and a wealth of designs, motifs, and symbols rich in hidden meaning. Here through the pottery of a long-standing civilization are conveyed some of its verities and mysteries, akin to those that have enveloped all past civilizations.

Part I sets forth the background of the subject and introduces it in a general way, while Part II treats the subject in greater detail, including technical data on paste and slip, style in form and decoration, type identification, pueblo of origin, and so on. The reproductions, in color and in black and white, illustrate points made in Part II and constitute a pictorial presentation of the subject.

The Pueblo Indians as Potters

When the Spanish explorers first entered the Southwest they discovered native peoples, widely diverse in physical type and material culture, who spoke different languages and lived in stone or mud-brick villages, or pueblos. Some of the Pueblo Indians lived in multistoried apartment complexes housing up to several thousand people in great harmony. The Spaniards found the Pueblo Indians to be clean, peaceful, generous, and to have a highly developed religion devoid of human sacrifice and organized warfare and stressing the importance of nature. It is hard to realize that these people, who attained one of the highest levels of Prehistoric culture in ancient North America, were hunters and gatherers a thousand years earlier. For, like many groups, struggling in isolated pockets of accelerated civilization a few thousand years earlier, these Stone Age people had discovered the advantages of community living, division of labor, controlled agriculture, and the techniques of craft work. They were Neolithic people, cultivating simple crops, using stone tools, and making pottery without the potter's wheel. What is impressive is that Pueblo pottery making had evolved to an advanced art, far beyond the stage of simple utilitarian wares, rivaling in artistry the finest Stone Age products of the Near East, northern and southern Europe, India, and China, created as much as six thousand years earlier.

One of the few Neolithic cultures to have created glazed pottery is that of the Pueblo Indians. The glaze paint, which has a glossy, melted appearance, was used only in the decoration. The technique virtually died out, however, shortly after 1700. Its place was taken by matte paint, derived from pigments obtained from local plants or finely powdered mineral substances. At the present day, decorated pottery is predominant among Pueblo wares, although plain and rough utility wares continue to be produced.

It is surprising how little the Europeans influenced the ceramic production of the Pueblo

Indians. Because of their innate traditional conservatism, Pueblo potters evolved a succession of styles that were remarkably independent of outside influence until the coming of the railroad about 1880, when wider markets provided a commercial stimulus for many of the pueblos.

Forms of Pueblo Pottery and Their Preservation

Bowls are vessels with an opening at approximately the greatest width, whereas jars have a proportionately much narrower opening and are usually taller. Large storage jars usually have a narrow mouth to facilitate coverage. Many of the older storage jars have a completely rounded bottom or at best a meager base. Of the various sizes of bowls the dough bowl is the largest, often capable of holding a week's supply of bread dough for a family. In general, Historic Pueblo bowls are scarcer than jars. Subject to cooking hazards and other domestic wear and tear, they have the more readily perished.

The large, heavy storage jars that held grain have come down through the generations as among the most plentifully preserved of all the pottery forms of the middle Historic period. This is because they remained relatively undisturbed in corners of back rooms. There, despite continuous service, they were not subject to dropping or other damage, for they were rarely moved.

One factor related to the preservation of these old storage jars and any other form of vessel that has managed to survive is the Indians' reverence for their pottery. Only completely shattered vessels were discarded. If possible, damaged pottery was mended or at least set aside in an unused corner. Many of the older vessels show homemade mending, such as holes drilled on either side of a severe crack and strung with rawhide or wire to pull the sides together. Sometimes rawhide thongs were wet and tied around the neck or body of a vessel so that when the rawhide dried it would tighten all the existing cracks.

Water jars, smaller and lighter than jars for storage, were used to scoop up water from a stream or river and to carry it back to the village. They usually have a concave base so that the vessel could be carried comfortably on top of the head, often without using the hands.

Canteens of all sizes are distinguished by their narrow necks, bulbous bodies, and two handles or knobs; when tied with rope or thong, these enable the vessel to be carried on the back or hung on a wall.

Pitchers have a handle on one side, possibly a spout on the other, and sometimes a tall neck. Rectangular pitchers with spouts for pouring were made, especially at Cochiti and Santo Domingo.

Ceremonial vessels and effigy figures in animal and human shapes are rare. They vary considerably in form and use. Certain tiny, narrow-mouthed jars have survived, and these are used to hold the sacred corn pollen. For the most part, greater care has been devoted to the preservation of ceremonial pottery than to domestic vessels. The most precious of all the vessels by virtue of their consecration, ceremonial ware was the least handled and usually remained carefully stored away. Among the most thoughtfully painted of Pueblo ceramics, such vessels came the closest to recording, as if in writing, the Indians' universe. Generally, ceremonial bowls are more exotic in their decoration than secular vessels, often covered with the sacred symbols of the Indians' religious traditions; these include human and animal figures, emblems of natural phenomena—lightning, rain, clouds—and depiction of mythological beings such as sky serpents.

With all early Historic Pueblo pottery it should be noted that the longer the period of use the more the surface takes on a smooth and mellow hand-rubbed look that differs considerably from that of a buried vessel of the same vintage. This lustrous patina can greatly enhance the esthetic appeal of fine Pueblo Indian pottery.

The Making of Pueblo Pottery

The method of making pottery is quite similar for all the Pueblo Indian types. The basic ingredient is clay, dug from a nearby deposit. After the raw material is finely pulverized and cleaned of all stones and other impurities, it is tempered with finely powdered material, such as volcanic ash, sand, or crushed potsherds. The type of tempering material varies among the pueblos, but the purpose is always the same. Temper keeps the wet clay from being too sticky and from cracking while the vessel dries; it is said to improve the strength of the vessel. In some cases, the tradition of using a certain type of tempering material may be related to ceremonial or religious matters. Each village is very conservative in adhering to its particular tradition, so that often it is possible to attribute a pot to a particular village on the basis of temper appearance alone.

To form a pot, no potter's wheel is used. The clay is rolled into short sections of "rope," and these are coiled to build up the walls. Thinning and shaping are then accomplished with a piece of gourd for a scraper. If the decoration is to be scratched or carved into the surface, this is the next step.

The surface of the body clay is quite rough, usually cannot be highly polished, and does not make a good base for painted designs. For these reasons, most decorated Pueblo pottery is covered with a slip. This is an especially fine red or white clay that is mopped on in a water suspension and then, while still damp, polished with a smooth stone or rag. In some areas (notably the Hopi pueblos) the basic clay itself can be nicely polished.

For many styles of Pueblo pottery, the underbody of the vessel is not slipped; the clay surface is smoothed as well as possible by a process called "floating." While the clay is still wet, the finest particles in it are puddled to the surface with a smooth stone. This produces a fine-clay coating that can be polished almost like slip. In some pueblos a contrasting color for the underbody is achieved with red or dark brown slip.

Black or dark decorations are produced by applying pigments made from the boiled juice of an appropriate plant, to which a powdered iron or manganese pigment may be added, depending on the traditions of each pueblo. A yucca paint brush usually was employed for this purpose. Red sometimes appears in the designs, again coming from the use of a red slip-like clay.

Firing is the next step. On a windless morning the vessels are laid out on a framework of rocks or sheets of metal. The entire group is covered with slabs of dried cow dung or other slow-burning fuel, which is set alight. The fire is smothered if the final color is to be jet black; otherwise the fire produces shades of tan, cream, red, orange, and yellow. Firing lasts for an hour or two, and the vessels are finished as soon as they are cool. Sometimes black scorched spots, called "fire clouds," form on the vessels; these blemishes are caused by the contact of pieces of burning fuel with the pots. Until very recent times no kiln was used for firing Pueblo pottery, and that convenience is still ignored by most modern Pueblo potters.

It is generally assumed that pottery making is purely women's work, just as weaving and embroidery are traditionally men's work among the Pueblo Indians (but not the adjacent Navajo). For at least a century, however, there have been many gifted artists among the Pueblo men who have been responsible especially for the painting of designs on pottery. More recently a few Pueblo men have been carrying out all steps in making pottery, with results that rival the best produced by the women. Circumstantial evidence suggests that men were traditionally the decorators of ceremonial pottery, even in the Prehistoric and early Historic periods, and may have also decorated some of the secular wares. This conclusion, based on the knowledge that many of the religious and ceremonial activities are performed only by men, is supported by a few tribal elders who have attested the decoration of pottery by men in the early nineteenth century.

Pottery Styles, Quality, and Trends

Anyone witnessing a major dance at Santo Domingo, Zia, or any other of the conservative pueblos sees that the entire village, not just the dancers, participates—preparing food, helping with ceremonial costumes and dress, and so on—and senses, too, the drain on each household for all kinds of needed articles. Until recently the Pueblo religion has been all-pervasive in every phase of village life and has been kept closed and secret from outsiders. Consequently, there is a great lack of recorded historical data. The relentless attempts of Europeans either to comprehend or to destroy Pueblo culture have been massively resisted. Even today's questions usually receive evasive answers from Indians.

There are good reasons to believe that much of the history of Pueblo Indian pottery was closely associated with secretly guarded Pueblo religious history, and to a large extent all pottery was considered sacred. The ability of the conservative Pueblo Indians to adhere tenaciously to their ancestral traditions is shown clearly in their pottery decoration. Feathers, volutes, star patterns, floral motifs, circles, clouds, suns, key motifs, and animal figures reveal how deeply the pueblos were centered in their own mythology. The "ceremonial break," a brief interruption of painted lines encircling virtually every Pueblo Indian vessel, is a traditional device that occurs from the twelfth century to the present. Its original significance is lost to us now. As one great religious center, the pueblos were responsive to one another. Among the pueblos themselves, religious symbolism and ideas crossed barriers of distance, time, and language, fitting into the spiritual needs of each individual village. Motifs and styles were freely borrowed. Often, pueblos known for certain desirable ceramic features traded their wares commercially. Some pueblos depended completely on others for particular types of pottery; Jemez, for example, after about 1700 imported its painted pottery principally from Zia.

Not all pottery styles were equally successful. Naturally there were peaks and valleys of artistic creativity, such as may occur in any culture. There were periods when styles of decoration became monotonous and static, as in the sixteenth century at virtually every Tewa pueblo. There were also periods of degeneracy when pottery standards were compromised. One example of poor manufacture occurred at Acoma in 1770–1830, when Acomita Polychrome was produced, though the preceding period and the following one showed a high level of ceramic artistry; this slump did not have a long-range effect on the high, overall quality of Acoma pottery. Of course, Pueblo pottery also reached peaks of excellence, as it did during the brilliant period of the early eighteenth century throughout most of the Pueblo area. Apparently, conditions were ripe at that time for such a cultural effervescence. Many factors can contribute to a cultural renascence—the introduction of a new slip or method of firing, the resettlement of a people, or the emergence of geniuses like Nampeyo of Hano (in the Hopi area) or Maria of San Ildefonso. Low levels of ceramic artistry can be altered by such catalysts as these, and a creative expansion may result. But, strangely, a pueblo's cultural depression does not necessarily need a catalyst to revitalize itself. Travails brought on by a harsh environment or enemy marauders have resulted in ceramic flowering. Such hardships can serve as a binding force, a cohesive element reinforcing Pueblo unity in time of danger, thus strengthening the Indians' desire to bring a closer harmony between mankind and the forces of nature and the gods; in this the perfection of pottery making is one important factor. Here again is a manifestation of the all-pervasive relationship between the Indians' ceremonial and secular lives.

A few general trends in Historic Pueblo pottery making may be noted, some widespread and general and some pertaining only to individual pueblos, although it must be understood that there are many exceptions and special cases. During the early eighteenth century there is a tendency for the sculpture of vessels to have one or several distinct flexures in vertical profile, usually occurring at the top or bottom of a band of decoration. There is also a widespread use of feather symbols as motifs. By 1760 both of these features were being abandoned. Both bowls and jars became very monotonous in their smooth contours at virtually every Southwest pueblo (except those in the northern Tewa area; see map). Jars became more nearly spherical, with but a short neck, while bowls became more nearly hemispherical. In style the decoration became more geometrical, with volutes predominating in the early nineteenth century, giving way to floral patterns as the century progressed. By 1870, another change in the form of jars took place: the appearance of a rather high shoulder (or position of maximum diameter). These and various other trends are discussed in more detail in Part II.

Pueblo Pottery Types and Dating

The evolution, correlation, and interrelationship of pottery types can be discovered only by a detailed study of the available evidence. By laboratory analysis of fragments from the vessels or pottery sherds of a given pueblo, it is possible to determine the mineral ingredients, paint pigments, and type of slip employed by that pueblo at a given period. Each pueblo area usually uses ceramic materials available only to its own group of villages. These attributes, with those of form and decoration, define what we call pottery "types." Each type is known by a two-part name (e.g., Powhoge Polychrome), and each is also characterized by a definite geographical distribution and period of manufacture.

Two essential factors relate to the dating of Pueblo Indian pottery types. The first is the remarkable fact that each pottery type is restricted to a relatively small area and brief time of manufacture; no style has ever been precisely repeated at some later date. The second is the availability of historical records concerning site or village occupancy, and of the tree-ring method of dating for determining the age of wood fragments and the associated pottery.

When primary evidence such as the existence of wood for tree-ring dating is lacking, usually there are sherds of pottery, traded from other pueblos, which can be recognized by the materials, paste, temper, slip, form, and style of decoration. Such associated trade-ware sherds of types that have been dated elsewhere form strong evidence for dating by association. The result is much evidence for dating by style; gradually a carefully documented compendium of stylistic features has evolved. Thus, Pueblo pottery types range themselves in chronological sequences that receive considerable confirmation according to evidence from tree-ring dating, from written records when available, and from a combination of fortunate circumstances of association.

Certain basic features of Pueblo pottery that relate to construction materials, shape (form), slip, and decoration, etc., are generally confined to a single period or area. Therefore these characteristics often prove helpful in distinguishing Pueblo pottery types and in indicating relations between them either in time or in trade movements.

Key Characteristics of Pueblo Pottery

Tempering Material. In making pottery the neutral material added to clay is called the temper. So persistent are the local traditions of tempering that the paste is one of the surest guides to place of origin. There are six basic tempering regions in the Pueblo area.

(a) Taos and Picuris: The temper is already in the clay; it consists of abundant flecks of micaceous crystalline mineral.

(b) The Tewa area: The decorated Tewa wares are tempered with finely powdered tuff, giving the appearance of fine grit. (Utility wares are tempered with the locally abundant crystalline rock.)

16

(c) Cochiti and Santo Domingo: The paste is Tewa-like, with a considerable amount of crushed crystalline rock and a softer white mineral.

(d) The central area: Zia, Santa Ana, San Felipe, Sandia, and Isleta all use much sand, usually water worn. Zia also includes distinctive bits of crushed volcanic basaltic lava or related dark semivitreous materials.

(e) The Acoma–Laguna–Zuni area: Here the temper is principally crushed pottery sherds. Laguna may also use rock.

(f) The Hopi area: The temper is usually not visible in the painted wares; sometimes finely powdered potsherds are included, and some types have considerable fine sand.

Variations and exceptions can be cited for every area, but these are relatively rare.

The Globular Jar Shape. Almost all pueblos have made jars with subspherical (globular) shapes. This simple form is a natural adaptation for purely useful purposes, and undoubtedly was developed independently many times. The only particularly significant occasion is associated with a strangely universal trend in the late eighteenth century to the abandonment of whatever sculptured form previously had been made and the adoption of a simple globular shape. The origin of this sudden and widespread change is not known, but by 1800 roundness was the trend at all major pottery-making pueblos but Santa Clara.

The Tewa Bowl Shape. This distinctive treatment appears to have been derived rather directly from a sequence of glaze-ware bowl shapes produced to the south and abundantly traded into the Tewa area (see map). The shape is simple, being essentially hemispherical except for an encircling concave band below the rim and separated from the underbody by a keel. While the style was locally popular and persisted (at San Juan) into the early 1900s, it was never widespread, examples being known only from along the Rio Grande. A variety of decorative treatments were used, including all-over black or red, or a red base with decorated concave band.

The Tewa Jar Shape. A distinctive shape for water jars originated in the Tewa area soon after the development of the concave base around 1550. A broadly flaring underbody, a midbody bulge below midheight, a tall neck gently tapering inward, and some degree of flaring at the rim characterize the form. The general style proved popular, and spread to many parts of the Pueblo area, usually along with the concave base. Of the major ceramic areas, only Acoma and the Hopi villages seem to have ignored it, although its influence at Zia and Zuni was relatively brief.

Slip Applied to Bases. Commencing about 1600, throughout the New Mexico pueblos, the underbodies of vessels were decorated with red slip. At Hopi pueblos this practice seems not to have started until about 1700, and after 1800 black slip was used at Zuni. Two basic arrangements have been employed. In the most common, the slip covers the base and extends part way up the side as far as the lowest encircling framing line. In the other, known as red banding, the slip is an unbroken red band around the vessel just below the lowest framing line.

From 1700 until 1920 or possibly later, red banding was common at Zia, Santa Ana, Cochiti, Santo Domingo, and the Tewa pueblos. It is also present on very late examples of Kotyiti Glazed Polychrome. One red-banded example from Laguna is known but it is apparently unique.

All other pottery areas used an overall red underbody, with the exception of Zuni, where, about 1800, there was a change to black (or very dark brown).

After 1920, red banding declined rapidly, being replaced by the all-over red treatment at all pueblos. Only at Zia and Santo Domingo do some old potters occasionally still use the red band. The principal dates for changeover are: Tesuque and San Ildefonso, 1915; Zia, 1928; Cochiti, 1935; Santo Domingo, about 1930.

Micaceous Slip. As compared with glaze, micaceous slip decoration has been less widespread, though more persistent. The pueblo center for this practice is at Taos and Picuris, where the paste itself is actually micaceous and no additional slip is used. The effect is that of a golden-bronze glitter. Some adjacent Tewa pueblos employed micaceous paste occasionally, but in most cases they used a nonmicaceous clay with sand temper for the basic vessel, with an added micaceous slip. Examples are known from Nambe, San Ildefonso, and Tesuque, which uses it even today. Recent experiments with micaceous slip have been tried at Cochiti with poor results, and at Santa Domingo, where at least one potter has achieved excellent results.

Glaze-paint Decoration. Glaze paint is glossy, vitreous, and has relief texture. No Pueblo Indian pottery has been completely glazed for waterproofing, but until 1700 the use of glaze paint for decoration was widespread. Glaze-paint decorations occurred sporadically (presumably accidentally) as early as 1000 A.D. The practice became consistently intentional in west central Arizona about 1250 and spread rapidly to Zuni and eastward, reaching the Rio Grande Valley by 1375.

An astonishing variety of styles subsequently developed. In the eastern (Rio Grande) area the technique culminated in Kotyiti Glaze Polychrome. At Acoma and Zuni, it culminated in Hawikuh Polychrome, which, especially at Acoma, represents the finest Pueblo pottery ever made. Shortly after 1700 the glaze-ware technique was lost, seemingly forever. Glaze on a jar with a concave base is rare.

Matte-paint Decoration. As opposed to glaze paint (which is glossy), matte paint is usually dull and flat. It has, however, been the dominant decorative medium since earliest times. Two basically different types were and are used, organic and mineral.

Organic paint is used for black decoration only. It is made by boiling down to a thick liquid the tender leaves and shoots of various plants, notably the Rocky Mountain bee plant, the paint from which is called guaco. The resulting decoration is usually a sooty black, often with a soaked-in appearance. The polished surface does not lose its sheen from use of purely organic paint.

Mineral paint is made by adding finely pulverized rock of appropriate type to a binder liquid, whereby various colors can be achieved, principally red, brown, yellow, and black. The last is distinguished from the black of organic paint usually by having a brownish or reddish tinge, sometimes by having a slight relief (not soaked in), and by being unpolished.

On Historic Pueblo pottery after 1700 organic paint was the principal black material at the northeastern pueblos of Nambe, San Ildefonso, Tesuque, Santo Domingo, and Cochiti, while mineral black was used at Santa Ana, Zia, Laguna, Acoma, Zuni, and the Hopi villages.

The "Ceremonial" Line Break. Continuing a tradition whose ancient origin is unknown, many of the pueblos have incorporated the line-break convention into the decoration of their pottery. Almost without exception the motifs on painted vessels are framed above and below with one or several encircling black lines. The line break, then, designates a short interruption or incompleteness in the framing lines of a band or a panel of decoration. Other names for the line break are "ceremonial break," and "spirit path," but these terms have implications that are not necessarily correct. While many theories have been advanced concerning the meaning of the line break, none can claim greater validity than any other; the *original* meaning is lost in antiquity (having originated at least a thousand years ago), and any modern belief, no matter how sincere, must be interpreted accordingly. Probably superstitious caution, like not walking under a ladder, serves most strongly to perpetuate the practice.

The pueblos that have most commonly employed the line break in recent history (after 1800) are Santo Domingo, Cochiti, Santa Ana, Zia, Laguna, Acoma, Zuni, and the Hopi villages. At Tesuque, it is extremely rare; at San Ildefonso, it is moderately rare. Taos and Picuris have used it in the punched or incised decoration of their micaceous wares. In the Tewa area, too, the line break was commonly employed on the earlier types from Sankawi Black-on-cream through Ogapoge Polychrome. At all localities, however, where use of the line break was common, there have been exceptions, occasional vessels having some or all of the framing lines complete.

The Feather Symbol. The album of illustrations is the best place to see the development and interchange of designs and motifs. One predominant feature, however, is of such widespread occurrence that it deserves special comment. As early as 1939, H.P. Mera emphasized the importance of the feather motif in its migration from the Hopi area eastward. Prehistoric Sikyatki pottery shows abundant use of the motif, as do the late Acoma and Zuni glaze wares. The most widespread occurrence, however, is early in the eighteenth century, when almost every Puname or Tewa vessel seems to have some form of feather symbol. Its occurrence is, in fact, a criterion for the identification of Ogapoge Polychrome. Series of feathers, split feathers, and triangular-capped feathers are all characteristic. Round-capped feathers also are common; omission of the cap is, at most pueblos, a later modification. Various adaptations and modifications have been used up to the present time.

Rim Top, Red or Black. Before about 1700, the rim tops of bowls and jars, if painted at all, were red in every major ceramic area. Apparently Acoma was the first pueblo to paint rim tops black, a change that occurred there shortly after the advent of matte-paint styles about 1730. A single black-rim sherd from Awatobi suggests that the practice was known in Hopi country before 1750. In the Puname area the change from red to black dates rather close to 1765, and it seems quite likely that by then the change had also occurred at Zuni. The Cochiti and Santo Domingo potters may have waited until as late as 1800 to change from red to black, but in this case the date is quite uncertain; by 1830 the change there was well established. In the Tewa area, red rim tops persisted until just after 1900; some polychrome jars from San Ildefonso with Cochiti slip have black rim tops, and the changeover was a distinct Cochiti influence. Once established in any area, the black rim tops seem to have persisted, making them useful in dating.

Fire Clouds. These are smudges of gray or black produced by the incomplete burning of fuel that has fallen against a vessel. From every Pueblo, one can see occasional examples. Black smudged pottery is an extreme case of intentional fire clouding. Certain pueblos almost invariably have fire-cloud blemishes; most prominent in this respect are Picuris and San Juan; Santa Ana vessels also are often fire-clouded.

Ring and Quality. The good ringing tone of a tapped vessel is almost universally regarded as an indication of quality. Actually, there are many criteria, subjective as well as objective, that contribute to the judgment of pottery excellence. There is fairly widespread agreement as to the superiority of Acoma ceramics. J.W. Fewkes (1898) was quite partial to the Prehistoric Hopi wares, and students of modern decor are generally great admirers of the recent polished black styles. The artistic (and other subjective) aspects can be argued endlessly; it is clear, however, that from the Indians' point of view certain features of serviceability are of particular importance. The ratio of volume to weight, for example, is of much significance for vessels that must be carried far. Strength and relative nonporosity are likewise important properties of good pottery. That the Indians also admire the artistic features, such as care in designing, use of color, absence of blemishes, etc., has often been observed.

What, then, does the nature of the ring tone contribute to the criteria of excellence beyond those features already mentioned? There is, of course, the subjective pleasure of a beautiful clear tone. Objectively, the ring tone can be characterized by four attributes: pitch, duration, overtone content, and beat intensity. Pitch is the dominant frequency of vibration; duration is the length of audible time after being struck; overtone content refers to the presence of minor frequencies in addition to the dominant one; beat intensity refers to the strength of throbbing in the tone. All of these properties are strongly variable, depending upon such features as wall thickness, hardness, size, symmetry, form, and integrity. (In this last respect, cracks or chips can often impair tone, but good tone does *not* necessarily mean the absence of cracks. A well-mended vessel may ring beautifully; there is an Acoma jar with a big crack in the base that rings well.)

Pitch is not necessarily a function of size alone; a large jar may have a higher pitch than a small one. The actual pitch does not seem to be correlated in any useful way with quality. Duration seems to be a more useful criterion; long duration seems well correlated with hardness.

Overtone is strongly associated with shape. The least content (purest tone) seems to be found in certain jars from Zia and Acoma. Beat intensity is closely related to symmetry. A jar with a strong beat intensity actually rings with two closely spaced dominant frequencies. Such a jar will produce beats only when struck at certain places around the side; at the in-between places the tone is pure.

Thus it can be concluded that the nature of the ring contributes little to the judgment of a vessel's quality. Occasionally a poor vessel with thick soft walls will ring nicely, while another with thin hard walls will have a poor ring tone.

PART TWO
Types of
Pueblo Pottery
of the
Historic Period

Northern Tiwa Pueblos

Picuris and Taos

Picuris and Taos have followed pottery traditions quite different from those of the other pueblos. Their utilitarian wares more closely resemble the nearby Apache pottery in being unpainted, unpolished, and decorated, if at all, only with such sculptural features as knobs, ribbons, or punching. The unpolished surfaces of the vessels were often intentionally roughened with combings or other striations, especially in the eighteenth and nineteenth centuries. Some were constructed by pressing the clay into baskets, thus producing a characteristic surface that looks as though a corncob had been rolled over it. For perhaps a century little pottery has been manufactured at Taos Pueblo, while Picuris Pueblo has been a ceramic leader and even today produces small quantities of serviceable pottery. The Tewa Indians sometimes copied the style of Picuris and Taos but used a different clay and temper. At Taos and Picuris the clay is formed of decayed pre-Cambrian schist, filled with abundant flecks of mica throughout, while the Tewa achieved the same metallic luster by coating their clay with a thick, glittery finish. The surrounding villages of Spanish-Americans have often used and appreciated the utilitarian pottery from Picuris and Taos. Picuris pots are characterized by their mottled appearance, which varies from glittery orange metallic to almost black, while Taos pots are often more uniform in color.

1
Picuris Jars and Pitcher
Left: 1750–1850. H. 35 cm. *Center:* 1955. H. 19 cm.
Both Coll. Francis Harlow. *Right:* 1890. H. 23 cm.
Coll. Mr. and Mrs. Larry Frank

The micaceous flakes that characterize Picuris
and Taos Pueblo utilitarian pottery show especially on the surface of the jar on the right and
in the metallic luster of the pitcher. The black
smudges on the pitcher are fire clouds. Two types
of native mending occur on the jar to the right:
wire around the neck and material plastered
over a crack. The jar on the left is decorated with
applied encircling clay ribbons.

Tewa Pueblos

Tewa pottery has always been distinguished by the use of vegetal paint for decorating vessels. In contrast to the mineral paint used in many of the other Pueblo areas, the vegetal black paint looks more soaked in, is more of a sooty black, and often retains the polished appearance of the slip. It is made from boiling the leaves and stems of the Rocky Mountain bee plant, from which the concentrated juice is dried into cakes called guaco.

By 1650, after the Indians had endured more than fifty years of Spanish rule, Tewa pottery underwent a major innovation. Previously all Tewa pottery had been decorated with black paint only; then the potters began experimenting with the use of red, and the results were sensational. Thus originated Sakona Polychrome (see figs. 4 and 5) and Tewa Polychrome (see color pl. I; figs. 6 and 7), which are landmark pottery types for the Rio Grande pueblo area. Jars of the former are decorated in a midbody band and on the neck area, whereas jars of the latter are decorated only on the midbody band, the neck being a beautiful polished red. New sculptural flourishes were added, including flaring rims on jars and sharply angular flexures on the bodies of bowls and jars. Both all-red and all-gray vessels were also made. The gray was achieved by firing the pottery in a reducing fire, in which little air is allowed to enter, so that a dense, smoky atmosphere surrounds each piece. By about 1720 the gray of the vessels was replaced by a beautiful black through the addition of a red slip before firing.

At that same time a split took place in the practice of ceramics in the Tewa area, a rift that was to last until the beginning of the present century. The northern pueblos of San Juan and Santa Clara turned to the production of unpainted red and black wares exclusively, while the southern pueblos of San Ildefonso, Nambe, Pojoaque, and Tesuque, followed a different course and manufactured some very beautiful painted pottery. Eventually, even the surviving southern pueblos turned principally to the production of the black and red wares: Nambe and Pojoaque about 1820, San Ildefonso about 1915, and Tesuque to some extent about 1920.

Santa Clara Pueblo

In the late classical period, up to about 1900, a great many excellent vessels were made at Santa Clara, all fired with the smudging technique that produces a fine black surface color. The bowls especially retained the classic eighteenth-century form, Santa Clara retained something unique form was duplicated at Pojoaque and Nambe. In contrast with San Juan traditions, where bowls especially retained the classic eighteenth-century form. Santa Clara retained something like the old styles for jars (see fig. 27). In sculpture these vessels eventually took on a unique Santa Clara look of their own, but much remained that was reminiscent of the old Tewa Polychrome form. In particular, the Santa Clara jars have a concave base (for carrying a vessel on the head), a widely flaring low underbody, a midbody bulge, and a rather tall, slender neck with a pronounced flare at the rim.

The departures from tradition are seen especially in the sculptural details that embellish a vessel. The rim is often rippled or fluted; the neck also may be rippled, with vertical or spiral carvings; and the midbody bulge may be sculptured. Before 1920 it was characteristic of the carved sculptural details to be as well polished as the rest of the surface and the depressions to vary smoothly from the adjacent area.

Especially distinctive is the "bear paw" sculpture, almost a Santa Clara trademark, which first appeared on vessels made in the latter half of the nineteenth century. This simple footprint motif is usually placed on jars in sets of three or more with no other decoration. Most impressive are the enormous storage jars, tall, ellipsoidal in form, with a short neck, and completely plain polished black except for three or four bear-paw imprints around the upperbody. The tallest approach 75 centimeters (29½ in.) in height and are accordingly the largest vessels ever made by Pueblo Indians.

Another ceramic form from Santa Clara is the wedding vase, which is a double-spouted jar with connecting handle.

If Santa Clara responded at all to the influence of the railroads in 1880, it was principally to increase the output of its widely famous black wares. But by 1900, with markets not widening appreciably and the pueblo's social unity gradually declining owing to increasing inroads of "civilization," Santa Clara's ceramic output was diminishing rapidly. All that was necessary to spark the modern revival was to observe the success at nearby San Ildefonso. There the black pottery previously traditional in Santa Clara was outmoded by the innovative new black-on-black technique of Julian and Maria Martinez. This sensational style combines a unique decorative feature (dull black decoration on a shiny black background) with a cooler than normal firing procedure capable of producing a much deeper black color. Soon Santa Clara Pueblo was again famous for its black wares.

San Juan Pueblo

Traditionally the pottery of San Juan has been plain polished red or polished black. Also traditional is the style of applying the polished slip, in either case to only the upper two-thirds of jars, and to only a band just below the rim on the exteriors of bowls. In both cases a line of demarcation between slip and paste can be clearly seen, with a resulting pattern of color that is pleasing. The rest of the surface is well-polished bare paste: a shade of orange-tan when the slip is red, and gray when the slip has been smudged black.

San Juan is the only Tewa pueblo that has consistently retained the early eighteenth-century form for bowls (see fig. 3). In fact, San Juan pottery of the classical period (before 1900) is quite traditional and has been little influenced by the coming of the railroads or the tourist trade. These traditional bowls are distinguished by an exterior profile that is convex over the base and lower slopes and concave in a band just below the rim. Between the convex and concave surfaces there is an angular keel, or bend, in the surface. On some relatively recent bowls the angular keel is replaced by a more rounded contour such as appeared much earlier at the southern Tewa pueblos.

Classically, San Juan jars are of two forms. One is nearly spherical, with a flat base and a very short neck. The other is similar, but flares to a wide opening almost as a bowl does. Both of these jar forms are either red, with orange-tan polished paste inside and on the exterior of the underbody, or black, with gray inside and on the exterior of the underbody. This latter style was also made at Tesuque and Cochiti, where decoration was painted on the exterior surfaces. Some very large and bulbous storage jars were made as late as 1900. These were used both locally and at other nearby villages, especially Taos. They are commonly black and gray in color.

Typical San Juan pottery is distinguished from that of Santa Clara by several consistent features. Santa Clara vessels dating before about 1920 are exclusively black in color; consequently those San Juan vessels that are red can be recognized with ease. Also, the slip applied to Santa Clara vessels often covers the entire vessel, and not just two-thirds of it. Other points differentiating San Juan from Santa Clara vessels are these:

1 San Juan vessels are usually thinner and lighter in weight.
2 Usually they have some very fine micaceous glitter on the unslipped surfaces, a feature almost never seen on Santa Clara vessels.
3 Often they are better polished on the interior of the vessel.
4 San Juan vessels were made in fewer shapes and forms, retaining the classical form for bowls, whereas Santa Clara produced numerous variants of the classical form for jars.
5 There are few sculptural details on San Juan jars, compared with Santa Clara jars.

I
Tewa Polychrome Jar

Circa 1690. H. 26 cm. Museum of New Mexico, Santa Fe, N.M., cat. no. 21864/11

Typical Tewa Polychrome features of this rare jar type are the midbody bulge, a strongly flaring rim, a concave base to facilitate carrying the vessel on the head, the red band on the underbody (begin-ning to narrow down to the thin width seen on later Pojoaque Polychrome; see fig. 12), the single framing lines bounding the midbody decoration, the zigzag band with dots, and the enclosed tri-angular-based F figures. The solid red upperbody contrasts colorfully with the austere black on white of Sakona Polychrome (as, e.g., in figs. 4 and 5).

II
Ogapoge Polychrome Jar
Circa 1750. H. 28 cm. University of Colorado Museum, Boulder, Colo., cat. no. 381

Typical for a late Ogapoge Polychrome jar, this vessel is less finely executed than the jar in figure 9. The underbody slopes are mostly convex, there is no sculptural or decorative differentiation of the midbody, and the framing lines are now heavy and double, all evolving towards the succeeding Powhoge Polychrome. The medallion motifs survive on Powhoge Polychrome in several variations, as in figure 15.

III
Pojoaque Polychrome Jars
Left: Circa 1725. H. 29 cm. *Right:* Circa 1725. H. 27 cm. School of American Research, Santa Fe, N.M., cat. nos. 2385/12 and 2384/12, respectively

Wide banding on the underbodies and single framing lines above and below decorative bands on the midbody show these jars to be relatively early examples of their type, closer in style to Tewa Polychrome than to later Powhoge Polychrome. The well-polished upperbodies are derived from Tewa Polychrome, but the motifs are distinctly different. In fact, the arc motifs are almost identical to those on the Pawohoge Polychrome storage jar in figure 14.

IV
San Ildefonso Polychrome Storage Jar

Circa 1890. H. 43 cm. Coll. Mr. and Mrs.
Larry Frank

Directly derived from the finest and most typical
storage jars of Powhoge Polychrome, this beautiful jar was made for service rather than the
tourist market by Mrs. Tonita Pena. The jar is
decorated in a style attributable to Alfredo Montoya. Red banding, red rim top, stone-polished
slip, native vegetal pigments, and all other details preserve the earliest traditions. It is virtually independent of outside influences.

V
San Ildefonso Black-on-red Storage Jar
Circa 1915. H. 47 cm. Coll. Mr. and Mrs.
Larry Frank

Although derived from the earlier Powhoge
Black-on-red (see fig. 35), this beautiful storage
jar is taller and differs from the earlier type in
the nature of the decoration. It utilizes a variety
of motifs derived from all parts of the Pueblo
world, modified and enhanced by the creative
imagination that was flowering at San Ildefonso
when this jar was made. Perhaps the most attractive features are the brilliant, well-polished slip
and the contrasting dense blackness of the decoration. The black rim top and the absence of red
banding join with the style of the decoration to
suggest the date of manufacture, which was near
the end of really exquisite stone-polished and
guaco-painted slip at San Ildefonso.

VI
Tunyo Polychrome Jar
Circa 1910. H. 26 cm. Coll. Robert Ashton

Extreme sculptural shape with thin hard-fired walls characterizes this jar as the product of Maria Martinez of San Ildefonso, with decoration by Julian Martinez, her husband. Typical of the early vessels by this couple, the surface is covered with rag-polished Cochiti slip. The red rim top and red-banded underbody are traditional features. The design consists of three birds hunting insects. Here is an example of the best of the commercially oriented San Ildefonso pottery made after 1900.

VII
Kiua Polychrome (Cochiti Variety) Storage Jar
Circa 1770. H. 38 cm. Coll. Mr. and Mrs. Larry Frank

Because of highly similar decoration, this outstanding storage jar of Kiua Polychrome may have been made by the same artist who made the storage jar in figure 61. Here the form is modified into the wide-mouthed variant restricted to Cochiti, San Juan, and Tesuque (as, e.g., in fig. 41). Like the one in figure 61, the vessel illustrated has a red rim top characteristic of Kiua Polychrome prior to 1800.

VIII
Kiua Polychrome (Cochiti Variety) Jar
Circa 1800. H. 48 cm. Coll. Mr. and Mrs. Dennis Hopper

Although the red rim top indicates a date of manufacture prior to about 1800, the style of decoration has evolved beyond that of color plate VII and figure 61, so that the date cannot be earlier than 1780. The unpainted (negative) leaf figures in the black corner embellishments are a common Cochiti pattern that persists from around 1780 to the present. The medallions are motifs common to both Kiua Polychrome and Powhoge Polychrome.

Kiua Polychrome Jar

Circa 1810. H. 43 cm. Coll. Mr. and Mrs.
Larry Frank

A striking pattern of hollow-stepped square
figures leads to horizontal stalks terminated by
feather "fingers," all these motifs reflecting
Tesuque and San Ildefonso influence (as, e.g.,
in figs. 18, 41, and 43). Keresan influence can
be seen in the sharp feather points and arc en-
closures. The simplicity and boldness of the
design, the width of the red band around the
underbody, and the strong ceremonial line-break
pattern are all Kiua Polychrome features. It is
difficult to establish whether this fine jar is of
the Cochiti or the Santo Domingo variety of
Kiua Polychrome.

X
Cochiti Polychrome Bowl
Circa 1930. Diam. 46 cm. Coll. Mr. and Mrs.
A. Edgar Benton

Red in the coloring of the decoration is somewhat unusual for Cochiti pottery. Otherwise, this large bowl is quite typical in form (with flaring rim), in the placement of the decoration (various isolated, unrelated items), and in its decoration (the sacred symbols that normally never appear on early secular pottery). The various cloud–rain–lightning symbols are very similar to those from Tesuque (as, e.g., in figs. 45 and 47–49). Some of the mythical creatures, however, are more typical of Cochiti in appearance (as, e.g., in fig. 87), and the curved, stepped spiral is distinctly of Cochiti origin (as, e.g., in fig. 63).

XI

Santo Domingo Polychrome Storage Jar
Circa 1915. H. 46 cm. Coll. Mr. and Mrs.
Larry Frank

An excellent example of Santo Domingo Polychrome, this storage jar differs from the older
Kiua Polychrome vessels from Santo Domingo
(as, e.g., in fig. 64) in having a more flaring rim,
isolated motifs not framed by paneling, naturalistic figures of birds, and a less conspicuous
underbody (giving a taller effect). Traditional
features are the red banding of the underbody,
the decorative pattern around the neck (as also
in fig. 64), and the top-to-bottom ceremonial
break through the right-hand motif. Materials,
construction, slip finish, and firing technique
show the more recent Santo Domingo pottery
at its best.

XII
Puname Polychrome Jar
Circa 1730. H. 23 cm. School of American Research, Santa Fe, N.M., cat. no. 3775/11

Resembling the Ashiwi Polychrome jar in color plate XXVI, this Puname Polychrome vessel is an outstanding example of the artistic qualities that have brought fame to early eighteenth-century Pueblo pottery. The rim top is red in the fashion typical of Zia pottery before 1765. Traits distinguishing this Puname jar from Ashiwi Polychrome (early Zuni) are the red arcs around the midbody, the red banding of the underbody, the sandy red paste tempered with black basalt fragments, and the different design embellish-

ments. The alternating wide and narrow four-panel arrangement of the decoration later became characteristic of Zia's San Pablo Polychrome.

XIII
Trios Polychrome Storage Jar
Circa 1800. H. 46 cm. School of American Research, Santa Fe, N.M., cat. no. 2508/12

This storage jar is either a late San Pablo Polychrome or an early Trios Polychrome example, having form and design characteristics of both periods. The bird figure similar to the bird's head in figure 100 is a Trios Polychrome innovation, as are the geometric figures on the side.

XIV
Trios Polychrome Storage Jar
Circa 1860. H. 39 cm. Coll. Mr. and Mrs.
Larry Frank

This rare, late Trios Polychrome storage jar has
evolved considerably from the one in color
plate XIII. The relatively naturalistic bird and
foliage indicate a late transitional stage from
Trios Polychrome to Zia Polychrome. The large,
bold bird surrounded by a rich patina contributes to the handsome appearance of the vessel.

XV
Zia Polychrome Ceremonial Jar
Circa 1890. H. 22 cm. School of American
Research, Santa Fe, N.M., cat. no. 3443/12

Few sacred ceremonial vessels from Zia Pueblo
have ever left that village. This one, with its
circular radiating sun figure, is the inspiration
for the design on the New Mexico state flag. The
cloud, lightning, and rain symbols were derived
from the same ideas that inspired the motifs in
figure 57. Triangular eyes are especially typical
of renderings of cloud faces at Zia and Tesuque
Pueblos. The dragonflies are related to earlier
bird figures (as, e.g., in fig. 100 and color pl.
XIII) at both Zuni and Zia.

XVI
Zia Polychrome Storage Jar
Circa 1910. H. 43 cm. Coll. Mr. and Mrs.
Larry Frank

This attractive large jar is representative of the fine storage jars that Zia potters were still making in the early 1900s. Strong but relatively thin walls, vigorous but graceful form, and excellent execution of the decoration are prominent features. The parrot and the deer motifs were widely adopted and modified in contemporary Pueblo pottery of the period.

San Ildefonso Pueblo

In contrast to the plain-ware tradition of the northern Tewa pueblos, the southern Tewa villages specialized in painted pottery throughout the Historic period (1600–1900). Until about 1730 the basic types were Sakona Polychrome and Tewa Polychrome (see above, Tewa Pueblos). In the following twenty years or more these gradually evolved into two excellent types, Ogapoge Polychrome and Pojoaque Polychrome (circa 1730–1760). Ogapoge Polychrome (see color pl. II; figs. 8–10 and 13) is decorated on both midbody and upperbody, always with abundant feather symbols, and incorporates red into the motifs. It may have been manufactured for sacred ceremonial purposes exclusively. Pojoaque Polychrome jars (see color pl. III; fig. 11) have a splendid polished, tall, red upperbody, a band of decoration on the midbody, and a red-banded underbody. A bowl is illustrated in figure 12.

After about 1760 the standard style for the area became the type known as Powhoge Polychrome (see figs. 14–29), named for the Indian designation for San Ildefonso. This pottery type is especially noted for the superb large storage jars that were made at San Ildefonso and Tesuque pueblos. Powhoge Polychrome jars are quite simple in form. The necks are relatively short, while the bodies are ellipsoidal or nearly spherical. Vessels of Powhoge Polychrome date from approximately 1760 to perhaps as late as 1880. They are decorated in black paint on a background of cream slip that extends one-half to three-fourths of the way down from the top. Below this the surface is polished bare paste, decorated only with a narrow dark red band at the upper edge. The black paint is carbon. It is used for the two (or more) bands of motifs, a narrow one just below the rim and a wider one (or two) below that. The bands have a double black line at top and bottom; sometimes this line is broken at one point on the circumference in a ceremonial break. The motifs in the narrow band are simple and geometric, while those in the wider band are more complicated and diversified. The motifs on Powhoge Polychrome, often geometric and involved, are striking and vary from crude to well executed. Bowls are usually painted on the exterior in a band just below the rim. Water jars are more common than bowls in San Ildefonso Polychrome pottery.

The rim tops of Powhoge Polychrome are always painted red, an important feature that aids in distinguishing these vessels from the Kiua Polychrome of Cochiti and Santo Domingo, where rim tops were painted black after about 1800. (There is, however, no red in the motifs of either Powhoge Polychrome or Kiua Polychrome.)

A principal problem in the identification of Powhoge Polychrome comes in distinguishing it from the more numerous Kiua Polychrome vessels. Kiua Polychrome is an offshoot of Powhoge Polychrome, made at Santo Domingo and Cochiti. The manufacture of Kiua Polychrome continued well after the last vessels of Powhoge Polychrome had been fired, so that it is a common mistake to identify wrongly the old Tewa vessels as early examples of Kiua Polychrome from the two Keresan pueblos to the south. There are basic differences that are summarized in the section describing Kiua Polychrome (see below). One characteristic, the ceremonial break, occurs occasionally on Powhoge Polychrome and frequently on Kiua Polychrome, and continues to be an attribute of later wares at Cochiti and Santo Domingo.

Both Powhoge Polychrome and Kiua Polychrome vessels had companion types that are quite rare. These are Powhoge Black-on-red (see figs. 33–35) and Kiua Black-on-red (see fig. 79). They differ in no way from their black-on-white cognates except for the use of rust-red slip as a background for the black designs.

At San Ildefonso the making of pottery declined considerably until by 1830 its decorated ceramic output was limited to large storage jars and a few smaller jars. Most small vessels were imported, principally from Nambe Pueblo, which received food and other items in return. This situation persisted until about 1880, when San Ildefonso pottery making underwent a tremendous revitalization, sparked by the influx of tourists arriving on the new cross-country railroad. Indeed, 1880 is reckoned as the earliest date for San Ildefonso Polychrome (see color pl. IV; figs. 30–32), the innovative new style that transformed Powhoge Polychrome into a commercially oriented product whose principal features were directed much more towards pleasing the customers' eyes than towards making a serviceable ware for domestic use. Continuing the tradition of stone polishing their vessels, the San Ildefonso potters re-established an old feature in their pottery making, that of incorporating red into the decoration of their creations. Concern for traditional motifs give way to new ideas, and the decoration of San Ildefonso Polychrome was more freely chosen from many sources for its artistic merit. Great variety plus considerable output attest to a San Ildefonso pottery renaissance. Conscious care was directed towards manufacturing attractive pottery for the general public. For example, the more graceful Santa Clara jar forms were adopted. At the same time, unfortunately, the vessels were sometimes fired at temperatures cooler than normal, presumably to avoid fire clouds, and the result was an inferior product from the standpoint of strength and utility. The pottery is often heavy, tending to be somewhat bulky, and sometimes is unable to hold water. But because of the prolific output of vessels in the brief period of their manufacture many more survived than one would likely expect. During this period the earlier tradition of producing black-on-red wares continued in a style known as San Ildefonso Black-on-red (see color pl. V; fig. 36). These paralleled the development of San Ildefonso Polychrome, but lasted through the 1920s.

By 1900 there was again a slump in pottery making at San Ildefonso. Only a few remaining potters, like the talented Martina and Florentino Montoya, Dominguita Pino, and the elder Tonita Pena continued to produce superb stone-polished wares. Market and output had fallen. By about 1907 there was a transition from the stone-polishing technique for polychrome wares to the rag-polishing technique that utilized a somewhat different slip material obtained from Cochiti. The stone-polishing process has the advantage of producing a more beautiful finish, but also is far more laborious. However, the Cochiti slip caught on, even though the San Ildefonso potters seldom completely mastered its use. Perhaps the expert rag-polishing craftsmen from Cochiti and Santo Domingo traded only inferior materials to their northern neighbors. Maria Martinez, the famous-to-be "Maria," began by using Cochiti slip, as did many of her contemporaries, and stone-polished local white slip has never again appeared. The results are sometimes beautiful, but more commonly are gray, streaked, and grainy. These San Ildefonso vessels with Cochiti slip, which differ from the earlier stone-polished San Ildefonso Polychrome, are known as Tunyo Polychrome (see color pl. VI), named for the prominent Tunyo Mesa just north of the village. The classic jar form of Tunyo Polychrome persisted to about 1915.

Production of modified forms of Tunyo Polychrome pottery continued to about 1925 and then was almost discontinued. Only the San Ildefonso Black-on-red ware retained the traditional stone-polished finish. The pottery craft at San Ildefonso was ripe for another renewal, needing only the catalyst of inventive and industrious persons. Maria and Julian Martinez met this need through the development of a new technique for decorating black pottery, a technique which was destined to bring them fame beyond that enjoyed by any other Pueblo potters and to revolutionize the craft at San Ildefonso as well as at nearby Santa Clara. Maria and Julian had served their apprenticeship in the early 1900s making Tunyo Polychrome vessels. About 1918 they found that if an unfired polished red vessel was painted with a certain mineral paint on top of the polish and then fired in a smudging fire at a relatively cool temperature the result would be a deep glossy black background with dull black decoration (see fig. 37). The new style was popular almost at once, and the subsequent prolific output found a ready market. Soon the successful technique was much copied, but Maria Martinez's family remained its master.

Throughout the Historic period of San Ildefonso pottery making a surprisingly large number of ceremonial bowls have been produced and have managed to survive the ravages of time. They have survived because of the infrequent use of ceremonial vessels as compared to the everyday use of domestic ware. Ceremonial pottery is also much better protected than domestic ware, since it has special meaning in religious ceremonies and is usually stored away in guarded places. The greatest number of ceremonial vessels preserved for us today come from San Ildefonso, Tesuque, and Zuni pueblos. In the last century San Ildefonso and Tesuque were the principal sources of excellent decorated sacred pottery for the other Tewa villages, where only a few plain-ware vessels were made for local ceremonial purposes. Various kinds of bowls evolved, some with terraced rims, some rectangular in form (at San Ildefonso), and some that are footed (especially at Tesuque). Their decoration includes such sacred symbols as clouds, rain, lightning, and other motifs of the firmament and nature, as well as clowns and the plumed serpent called Avanyu, a mythological sky creature. True ceremonial vessels are some of the most artistic and most treasured vessels the Pueblo Indians made.

Unfortunately, along with these vessels, San Ildefonso produced from 1915 to 1925 a number of pseudo ceremonial vessels made for non-Indians. This did not occur at Tesuque, where ceremonial pottery remained traditional.

Tesuque Pueblo

The examples of Powhoge Polychrome made in Tesuque in the late 1700s and early 1800s (see figs. 38–43) are at least as fine as those from San Ildefonso, and in some cases they are perhaps even more artistic and better made. The decoration is both vigorous and sensitive in execution, usually carried out with sure command. These stone-polished Tesuque vessels of Powhoge Polychrome are distinguished from those of San Ildefonso by having flatter bases, more ripply surfaces, occasional crystalline rocks in the paste, and a somewhat different style of design, as shown in the illustrations.

Around 1830 the Tesuque variety of Powhoge Polychrome evolved into Tesuque Polychrome (see figs. 44–47 and 50–54), and this beautiful type was popular from that time until as late as 1910. Almost the finest examples of this period of Tesuque pottery are the ceremonial vessels, which are often footed. Tesuque vessels were used in Spanish-American homes in Santa Fe and also were exported to the pueblo of Pecos, and yet, prior to about 1910, Tesuque styles evolved seemingly without reference to non-Indian influences. Perhaps it was the Tesuque Indians' conservatism that kept them making their own vessels while commercial products were being produced at the other pueblos. Even the tremendous San Ildefonso revival in 1880 exerted relatively little influence—principally the occasional addition of red to the decoration.

This stone-polished Tesuque pottery with the addition of red (or sometimes pale blue) is called Tatungue Polychrome (see figs. 45, 55, and 56). It was produced side by side with the usual black-on-white Tesuque Polychrome vessels, only for some reason it is exceedingly rare. Both Tesuque Polychrome and Tatungue Polychrome effectively ended around 1910. In general a similar deftness of drawing and a handsome slip prevailed on Tatungue Polychrome as on the Tesuque vessels of the past.

It is possible to distinquish Tatungue Polychrome from the contemporaneous San Ildefonso Polychrome not only by means of the same criteria that separate the earlier Tesuque Polychrome from Powhoge Polychrome but also by the additional fact that the red paint of Tesuque is often not edged with black, whereas at San Ildefonso the black is almost invariably present as an edging to the red.

Finally, traditional Tesuque pottery began to decline both in quantity and in quality with little of value produced after the early 1900s. Instead, there was a prolific output of decadent tourist-oriented wares, pots and figurines that were fired before being painted and then decorated in a profusion of bright poster-paint designs.

Nambe Pueblo

Until about 1830 Nambe Pueblo was a tremendous center for the manufacture of painted pottery. The style, which closely resembles Powhoge Polychrome, is called Nambe Polychrome (see figs. 58–60). The features distinguishing Nambe Polychrome from Powhoge Polychrome and Tesuque Polychrome are:

1 The relative abundance of coarse mica flakes (usually over 1.0 millimeter in diameter) on the exposed surfaces of paste, resulting from the close proximity of Nambe to the granitic Sangre de Cristo Mountains.
2 The use of relatively thin and soft white slip.
3 Occasional embellishment of the space between paired panel lines with simple motifs.
4 Relatively sloppy execution of the decoration.

Otherwise, Nambe Polychrome closely resembles its contemporaneous neighboring types. Part of the reason for the degeneracy of Nambe Polychrome may be attributable to its mass production for export. Abundant evidence exists to show that Nambe was a major trading center, with pottery serving as a medium of exchange for food and other goods at the neighboring

Indian pueblos and Spanish haciendas, as well as at Santa Fe. Fragments of pottery are more abundant at Nambe than at any of the other Tewa pueblos, and the characteristic Nambe features are also seen on a high percentage of the sherds found at nearby settlements. In addition, the traditions related by old-timers from El Rancho, a Spanish settlement near San Ildefonso, show that they and the San Ildefonso Indians were repeatedly visited more often by Nambe traders than by traders from any of the other nearby Indian villages. The Nambe Indians usually walked carrying pottery tied to their backs "in big white blankets." This observation, together with the finding of Nambe sherds at other pueblos, indicates that only relatively small bowls and jars were traded. Large storage jars and dough bowls were made at each village only for local use.

Around 1830 the production of decorated wares at Nambe decreased sharply, and it is likely that none were made at that village thereafter. Production of decorated wares, except for storage jars and ceremonial vessels, nearly ceased at San Ildefonso also, and may have been somewhat curtailed at Tesuque. Perhaps the opening of trade routes from the United States, via the Santa Fe Trail, at that time reduced the local Spanish demand for decorated Indian pottery. The Indians themselves could get along with simple utilitarian wares, for which there continued to be brisk trade among the pueblos, with Nambe still a major source until as late as 1860.

These later Nambe vessels consist principally of black wares, with fluted-rimmed bowls like those of Santa Clara, micaceous-slip jars superficially resembling the vessels from Picuris, and plain tan vessels of relatively rough finish. By 1880, however, pottery manufacture had decreased to such a point that James Stevenson received no inkling of the previous importance of Nambe as a ceramics center. Nevertheless, traditional utility wares and black pottery continued to be manufactured occasionally at Nambe until as late as 1950.

2
Santa Clara Jar

Circa 1890. H. 31 cm. Coll. Francis Harlow

This classic form of Santa Clara Black pottery
retains a modified version of the ancient Tewa
pottery shape (as, e.g., in figs. 4 and 5). Notice
three sculptured areas: the fluted rim, the raised
ridge at the base of the neck, and the carved
bear paw. The bear paw has been a common
Santa Clara motif since 1850. The surface, including the interior of the rim, is a glossy black.

3
San Juan Bowl

Circa 1900. Diam. 30 cm. Coll. Francis Harlow

The shape of this bowl remains essentially un-
changed from eighteenth-century forms of Tewa
pottery. The most recognizable features are the
thick red slip on the upper concave area, the
unslipped underbody, and the typical fire clouds.
The interior also has a nicely polished unslipped
surface.

4
Sakona Polychrome Jar
Circa 1680. H. 28 cm. Coll. Francis Harlow

This fine old jar and the one in figure 5 are the only two fairly complete Sakona Polychrome jars known to the authors. The sculptured form consists of several strong flexures and a sharply outflaring rim. The triple lines around the top and middle were replaced by 1700 by single lines framing the decoration. By 1760 the single lines were doubled and so remained until 1930. The motifs are placed in a narrow midbody band and a wider band on the upperbody. Red appears on the rim top and in a wide band on the lower underbody; no red is used in the motifs. The derivative type is Ogapoge Polychrome (see fig. 9). Although the styles of the two types are quite similar, Ogapoge Polychrome has red in the motifs and usually an abundance of feather symbols.

5
Sakona Polychrome Jar
Circa 1700. H. 18 cm. University of Colorado Museum, Boulder, Colo., cat. no. 381

Although there is no red in the decoration, except on the rim top and the underbody, the jar shown here differs from the one in figure 4 in the use of single framing lines, the abundant feather symbols, the midbody paneling, and the somewhat narrow form. This jar is therefore transitional between Sakona Polychrome and Ogapoge Polychrome. After the Spanish reconquest of the Pueblos in 1694 Indian refugees took this jar with them when they joined the Navajo at Gobernador Canyon.

6
Tewa Polychrome Bowl

Circa 1690. Diam. 33 cm. Museum of New Mexico, Santa Fe, N.M., cat. no. 11/16834

Typical in form for Tewa Polychrome (see fig. 7), this crudely executed bowl shows a rare example of Spanish influence in the circular motifs, probably derived from Spanish Majolica vessels of this period. The pair of zigzag lines with dots inside is a standard Indian device.

7
Tewa Polychrome Bowl

Circa 1690. Diam. 39 cm. Museum of New Mexico, Santa Fe, N.M., cat. no. 4423/11

A landmark piece, this Tewa Polychrome bowl has a slightly concave area of decoration, a strongly incurved convex underbody, and a sharply angular keel separating the two. The decoration is simple for the period. Persistence of this form of bowl is shown in figures 21 and 112, the latter indicating that the style is widespread among the Rio Grande pueblos. Even later bowls show the persistence of this form at San Juan (as in fig. 3), and Tesuque (as in fig. 55). Perhaps the most beautiful adaptation is exemplified by the Trios Polychrome bowl in figure 102.

8
Ogapoge Polychrome Ceremonial Jar
Circa 1760. H. 11 cm. Coll. Francis Harlow

This sacred ceremonial jar was made at a time when the Spanish were trying hard to discourage "pagan idolatries" and win converts to the Catholic faith. The vessel was long kept hidden and called into service only on selected and guarded occasions. Each element of the decoration is significant. In the center is an altar, with black steps on the left and red-filled steps on the right, said to portray night and day. From each lower corner hangs a cluster of four feathers, alternating red and black in their bodies and caps. Four zigzag lightning symbols are attached to the altar. In those days it is likely that these symbols played the dual role of lightning and serpent, which are closely allied sky deities. The little motifs near the handles are interpreted as rain clouds.

9
Ogapoge Polychrome Jar
Circa 1730. H. 28 cm. School of American Research, Santa Fe, N.M., cat. no. 3935/12

Typical form and decoration and abundant feather symbols with black and red fillings characterize this handsome Ogapoge Polychrome jar. The midbody decorative band has almost completely faded.

10
Ogapoge Polychrome Storage Jar
Circa 1740. H. 39 cm. Museum of New Mexico, Santa Fe, N.M., cat. no. 12519/12

This fine old vessel is the only known Tewa storage jar dating before 1750. Its form is helpful in recognizing the earliest Powhoge Polychrome storage jars (see figs. 14 and 15). The motif of stalks bearing feathers may be compared with the feather motifs on the following two less delicately executed Pojoaque Polychrome vessels. The midbody band is hardly discernible. A narrow red band at the jar's base and a well-floated convex underbody and base suggest that the vessel was manufactured at San Ildefonso.

11
Pojoaque Polychrome Jar
Circa 1720. H. 29 cm. University of Colorado
Museum, Boulder, Colo., cat. no. 380

Pojoaque Polychrome is very similar to Tewa
Polychrome, but differs in the relatively greater
width of the midbody and in the motifs, here
feather symbols. In this typical example the
beautifully polished red upperbody is like that
on the two Pojoaque Polychrome jars in color
plate III. Single framing lines around the band
of decoration occur frequently on Tewa Polychrome, Pojoaque Polychrome, and Ogapoge
Polychrome. This contrasts with as many as
three framing lines on the earlier Sakona Polychrome and two framing lines on the later
Powhoge Polychrome.

12
Pojoaque Polychrome Bowl
Circa 1750. Diam. 31 cm. Museum of New
Mexico, Santa Fe, N.M., cat. no. 21880/11

Earlier examples of Pojoaque Polychrome have
a sharper angle at the bottom of the area of
decoration and a less inflated underbody. In
design this bowl is quite typical of Pojoaque
Polychrome. Notice that the red band around
the middle has become quite narrow and persists
this way on Tewa pottery until well after 1900.

13
Ogapoge Polychrome Storage Jar
Circa 1760. H. 46 cm. Museum of New Mexico, Santa Fe, N.M., cat. no. 16117/12

This fine storage jar represents either a very late stage of Ogapoge Polychrome or a very early stage of Powhoge Polychrome. A slight reddish tinge in the arcs on the feather caps makes us classify it as Ogapoge Polychrome. The use of one framing line at the bottom and two framing lines at the top of the decorated area indicates the transitional nature of the jar. Evolving from the style exemplified in figure 10, this vessel shows relative boldness and lack of delicacy in execution, absence of the narrow lower band of decoration, and a more nearly spherical form. The rounded base and the well-floated under-body slip suggest that the jar was manufactured at San Ildefonso.

48

14
Powhoge Polychrome Storage Jar

Circa 1770. H. 51 cm. Museum of New Mexico, Santa Fe, N.M., cat. no. 16616/12

The double framing lines and globular shape identify this large storage jar as Powhoge Polychrome. Decorative motifs are arranged in three bands. The feather symbols were inherited from Ogapoge Polychrome, and the arcs with cresting black triangles come from Pojoaque Polychrome. Although the framing lines have no ceremonial breaks, the rounded and well-polished underbody and white flecks in the paste suggest that San Ildefonso is more likely than Tesuque to be the pueblo of origin.

15
Powhoge Polychrome Storage Jar

Circa 1780. H. 40 cm. Coll. Mr. and Mrs. Larry Frank

In comparison with later examples of the type, a less spherical form (as in fig. 10) indicates an early date for this Powhoge Polychrome storage jar. San Ildefonso traits are suggested by the round, well-floated underbody, in contrast to the flattened base usually seen on Tesuque vessels. The isolated medallion on the left is seldom seen on Tewa pottery after 1800–1820. The capped and rounded feather motifs are traditional. When their tips are broken into three

caps, a relationship to rain-cloud symbolism is indicated. The lustrous patina from many years of use has imparted much beauty to this remarkable vessel.

16
Powhoge Polychrome Storage Jar

Circa 1800. H. 53 cm. Museum of New Mexico, Santa Fe, N.M., cat. no. 41807/12

The feather symbols and checkerboard pattern on this storage jar are reminiscent of the decorative elements on the storage jar illustrated in figure 14. The nearly spherical shape of this later vessel, the double framing lines, and the arrangement of the motifs in the bands of decoration all are typical of the period. In the motif on the left four leaf-like elements remain unpainted in a negative style that was to become a feature of Cochiti pottery until modern times (as, e.g., in figs. 18, 63, 65, 84).

17
Powhoge Polychrome Storage Jar

Circa 1800. H. 48 cm. Museum of New Mexico, Santa Fe, N.M., cat. no. 12245/12

This storage jar is so nearly like the one in figure 16 that we suspect they were made at approximately the same time, perhaps even by the same potter. The red banding just below the decoration is wider than usual.

18
Powhoge Polychrome Storage Jar
Circa 1800. H. 39 cm. Coll. Mr. and Mrs.
Larry Frank

San Ildefonso features visible on this venerable,
mellow storage jar are the well-smoothed underbody, the small support area, or base, and the
lacy style of decoration. The narrow red band
at the top of the underbody and the watery, thin
quality of the black paint contrast with the contemporary style of Kiua Polychrome made at
Santo Domingo and Cochiti twenty miles to the
south, where the red band is wide and the paint
quite black (as in fig. 65). A contrast in the slip
is also evident; this Powhoge Polychrome storage
jar has a softer surface appearance than those
of Kiua Polychrome. Somewhat unusual is the
double band of decoration near the mouth.

19
Powhoge Polychrome Storage Jar
Circa 1820. H. 44 cm. Coll. Mr. and Mrs.
Larry Frank

The narrow band of decoration at the neck contains a motif that became immensely popular on
Kiua Polychrome, especially at Santo Domingo.
The isolated medallions in the larger band on
this striking storage jar become rare in Powhoge
Polychrome after about 1820. The narrow mouth
makes it easy to cover the jar to protect the dry
grain stored within. San Ildefonso characteristics
are the well-floated underbody and the rounded
base.

20
Powhoge Polychrome Jar

Circa 1800. H. 21 cm. Museum of New Mexico,
Santa Fe, N.M., no. 12354/12

Negative decoration is not unusual at San Ildefonso where this small jar was made. Positive
versions of much the same midbody pattern are
shown in figures 22, 23, and 24. The narrow
band at the neck contains a motif that has been
used from prehistoric times to the present in
either negative or positive form (as, e.g., in figs.
18, 59, 107, 127, 128).

21
Powhoge Polychrome
and Kapo Black Bowls
Left: Circa 1780. *Right:* 1780–1880. Diam. 23 cm.
Coll. Francis Harlow

In form these two small bowls show direct
descent from Tewa Polychrome (as, e.g., in figs.
6 and 7). The San Ildefonso painted bowl has a
motif in common with the vessels in figures 22
and 23. Framing lines above and below the
decoration show ceremonial breaks.

The Kapo Black bowl is thin, light, and well
fired. Large flakes of mica visible on the surface
indicate that it originated at Nambe.

22
Powhoge Polychrome Water Jar
Circa 1830. H. 24 cm. Coll. Mr. and Mrs.
Larry Frank

Notice the remarkable similarity of this vessel
to the one in figure 23. Both vessels could have
been made by the same potter, or at least decorated by the same painter at San Ildefonso. This
is a very characteristic Pueblo water jar; the
base is concave to facilitate carrying the vessel
on the head, and a red band is visible above
the well-floated underbody. The stone-polished
Tewa white slip is hard and fine, and the decoration is executed in dense carbon paint, derived
from the boiled leaves and stems of the Rocky
Mountain bee plant. The rim top is red, as required by Tewa traditions until 1910.

23
Powhoge Polychrome Jar

Circa 1830. H. 34 cm. Museum of New Mexico,
Santa Fe, N.M., cat. no. 45611/12

The rounded base and well-polished underbody
indicate a San Ildefonso origin for this boldly
decorated jar (for a very similar jar, see fig. 22).
A leather strap, tied around the neck, serves the
purpose of holding some minor cracks together.
The narrow red band at the top of the underbody
contrasts with the wide red band found on similar jars of Kiua Polychrome (as, e.g., in fig. 67).

24
Powhoge Polychrome Storage Jar
Circa 1810. H. 44 cm. Museum of New Mexico, Santa Fe, N.M., cat. no. 12170/12

Here again is a variant of the decorative style illustrated in figures 23 and 60. The red band at the top of the underbody is unusually wide for Powhoge Polychrome. Characteristic features of both Nambe and San Ildefonso wares are shared by this storage jar, confirming the close ties felt between those villages at this period.

25
Powhoge Polychrome Storage Jar
Circa 1870. H. 43 cm. Coll. Mr. and Mrs. John Painter

The lacy style of the motifs shows that this storage jar belongs to the later period of Powhoge Polychrome at San Ildefonso. The feather symbols are a holdover from earlier styles, like those of figure 16. The curving vine in the upper narrow band shows considerable relaxation of the older formality of treatment for this area. Tesuque vessels of this period are even more commonly embellished with wavy lines of this sort (as, e.g., in fig. 51).

26
Powhoge Polychrome Jar
Circa 1880. H. 26 cm. Museum of New Mexico, Santa Fe, N.M., cat. no. 18840/12

The rather tall neck and the pendent scallops,

suggesting Cochiti and Tesuque influence, and the little clown figures (*K'ossa* figures) with sashes hanging between their legs all indicate a relatively late date for this jar from San Ildefonso. These clowns are usually found only on sacred ceremonial pottery, of which this jar may be an example. The key motifs, or split stepped motifs, alternating with the clowns also occur chiefly on sacred pottery until around 1880, after which they appear frequently on the secular wares from San Ildefonso (as in fig. 30).

27
Powhoge Polychrome Rectangular Bowl
Circa 1880. 17x10 cm. School of American Research, Santa Fe, N.M., cat. no. 11152/12

This rectangular bowl teems with sacred motifs from Pueblo Indian mythology. On the interior are the head and shoulders of the sacred clown (see also figs. 26 and 29). The adjacent crossed lines are usually identified as a star. At the left on the exterior is a degenerate version of the age-old plumed serpent, called Avanyu, brother to the lightning and important in rain-seeking ceremonies. Above and below the serpent are triple arcs representing cloud banks. From the higher of these, rain falls (the short lines below) while lightning strikes in the form of zigzag lines ending in arrowheads. A larger bank of clouds is seen on the interior at the right, while the exterior at the right has a cloud bank supported by a triangular base, a common feature at Cochiti, Tesuque, and other Rio Grande pueblos.

28 & 29
Powhoge Polychrome Rectangular Bowl
Circa 1880. 12x22 cm. Museum of New Mexico, Santa Fe, N.M., cat. no. 11153/12

This rectangular bowl, similar to the bowl in figure 27, includes on the interior the sacred clown, important as a human impersonation in Pueblo ceremonies and sacred dances. On the sides of the interior are numerous stars (the criss-cross lines) and a plumed serpent, the latter in an ancient and traditional form. A plumed serpent also occurs on the exterior, along with stars and massive banks of clouds. At the left on the exterior is a cornstalk, with an ear of corn and a tassel, a feature often painted on sacred vessels of the Rio Grande pueblos. The rim top is decorated in black carbon paint.

30
San Ildefonso Polychrome Water Jar
Circa 1905. H. 25 cm. Coll. Francis Harlow

Three features mark this San Ildefonso Polychrome water jar as distinctly different from the previous styles of Powhoge Polychrome: the tall neck; the red in the decoration; the imaginative innovations in the motifs. Traditional features are the well-floated underbody with a concave base and a narrow red band at the top, the mellow stone-polished look, the designs painted with guaco and red clay, and the red rim top. Maria Martinez, the famous San Ildefonso potter, fashioned this jar, and her husband, Julian, painted it. This is the only known example of stone-stroked San Ildefonso Polychrome by the couple; all of their other polychrome vessels have rag-polished Cochiti slip.

31
San Ildefonso Polychrome Water Jar
Circa 1900. H. 28 cm. Coll. Francis Harlow

An excellent example of San Ildefonso Polychrome, this water jar was made by Martina and
Florentino Montoya, gifted potters who carried
on traditional pottery-making techniques much as
their ancestors did. Unusual for San Ildefonso
water jars are the black rim top, the extension of
the white slip clear to the base, and the wide
black bands at the shoulder and the top of the neck.

32
San Ildefonso Polychrome Jar
Circa 1900. H. 27 cm. Coll. Mr. and Mrs.
Larry Frank

Another splendid example of Martina and Florentino Montoya's work, this jar combines light
weight and serviceability with artistic excellence
in a pottery type that was often somewhat sloppy
in appearance and poorly fired. Martina carried
out the basic construction, and Florentino painted
the decoration. The black rim top and pendent
arcs around the neck are Cochiti embellishments.
The neck has an interesting motif on the interior, but the underbody is treated traditionally
(unslipped and red banded).

33
Powhoge Black-on-red Water Jar
Circa 1840. H. 21 cm. Coll. Francis Harlow

This rare little water jar of Powhoge Black-on-red appears to have been made in Tesuque. The medallions are filled with motifs like those in figure 20; they also resemble the medallion on the jar in figure 15. Compared with the red slip on the jar in figure 35, the red slip on this example is much thinner, although both have the same orangy tint.

34
Powhoge Black-on-red Jar
Circa 1880. H. 19 cm. Coll. Mr. and Mrs. Larry Frank

This little jar of Powhoge Black-on-red, also probably from Tesuque, closely resembles the jar in figure 33; especially in form, color, and layout of the decorated areas. It differs mainly in being more squat in form, in having a ridge within the neck (to hold a lid, now lost), and in the motifs, which are based almost exclusively on three types of feather symbols. The decoration on the interior shows an interesting persistence of a much older motif (as, e. g., in figs. 38 and 39). Black dots on the rim top are more often seen on ceremonial vessels (as, e. g., in figs. 47 and 49), and this jar may have been used for such a purpose.

35
Powhoge Black-on-red Storage Jar
Circa 1900. H. 37 cm. Coll. Francis Harlow

Dominguita Pino of San Ildefonso made this traditional Powhoge Black-on-red storage jar. For forty years Mrs. Pino and her daughter were important in creating these red wares. A trait in common with the late nineteenth-century jars, especially at Tesuque, is a ridge within the neck for supporting a lid. The usual form for such a lid is dome-shaped, with a handle in the center, also made of pottery and decorated with motifs in black on red. The Indians' traditional method of mending cracks is well illustrated here.

36
San Ildefonso Black-on-red Water Jar
Circa 1905. H. 23 cm. Coll. Francis Harlow

Like the storage jar in figure 35, this San Ildefonso Black-on-red water jar also was made by Dominguita Pino. Though several traditional traits have been eliminated, it is in the style of San Ildefonso Polychrome, with a shape newly borrowed from nearby Santa Clara Pueblo. Notice the extremely narrow underbody, surmounted by a broad middle body and nearly vertical neck. Indicative of a late date are the black rim top, a Cochiti trait introduced by the Montoyas (see figs. 31 and 32), the decoration within the rim (see also fig. 32), and the absence of a red band below the decorated area (see also fig. 31).

33

34

60

37

San Ildefonso Black-on-black Storage Jar

Circa 1935. H. 48 cm. Museum of New Mexico, Santa Fe, N.M., cat. no. 31959/12

This enormous storage jar illustrates the artistic style that brought fame to Maria Martinez of San Ildefonso and her husband, Julian, who painted the decoration. How to make and fire a dull black on shiny black was discovered about 1918, and the style has persisted to the present at San Ildefonso and also at Santa Clara, and in a some-what degenerate modification at Santo Domingo. Although this couple had earlier made poly-chrome vessels (see fig. 30 and color pl. VI), it is the black wares for which they are famous. Little of traditional design remains and service-ability is poor, all being sacrificed in the name of beauty and artistry. In this case the incentive for such innovation was commercial, and the results have been resoundingly successful.

38

Powhoge Polychrome (Tesuque Variety) Storage Jar

Circa 1820. H. 28 cm. Museum of New Mexico, Santa Fe, N.M., cat. no. 12169/12

Both the roughly finished underbody and the style of decoration indicate that this Powhoge Polychrome storage jar is of the Tesuque variety. The particular pattern used here in the nar-row neck band appears only on vessels dating before 1825.

39

Powhoge Polychrome (Tesuque Variety) Storage Jar

Circa 1800. H. 33 cm. Coll. Mr. and Mrs. Larry Frank

Many features of the decoration on this exqui-site jar are like those on the jar in figure 38, including the pattern in the narrow neck band and the elements on the periphery of the medal-lion on the right. Two additional features of Tesuque design are the radiating feather cluster

within the medallion (see also fig. 43) and the set of sharp prongs on the medallion at the left (see also fig. 40). Other indications of Tesuque origin are the dimpled appearance of the slipped surface, especially at the left, the dull finish for the underbody, the lopsided shape, and the absence of ceremonial breaks in the framing lines.

40

41
Powhoge Polychrome (Tesuque Variety) Bowl

Circa 1840. Diam. 49 cm. School of American Research, Santa Fe, N.M., cat. no. 2809/12

The form of this large bowl occurs principally at San Juan, Cochiti, and Tesuque. Decorative motifs indicating that the vessel was made at Tesuque are: the hollow rectangular areas; the radiating feather clusters (see also fig. 39); and the tall key motifs. The triangular supporting base for either a feather cluster or a double key also occurs on San Ildefonso pottery of the early nineteenth century. Even bowls have the traditional two-band arrangement of the decoration. Note the typical Tesuque dimpling on parts of the slipped surface. This bowl has been mended with strips of coarse wet leather to pull the cracks together when the leather dried.

40
Powhoge Polychrome (Tesuque Variety) Storage Jar

Circa 1830. H. 53 cm. School of American Research, Santa Fe, N.M., cat. no. 2465/12

This beautiful jar is one of the tallest vessels of painted Pueblo Indian pottery ever made. The white (negative) rectangles in the black areas on the left, the spiky crown-like motifs pointing upwards and downwards on the right, and the feather-like "fingers" on the far right (see also fig. 43) are features of Tesuque design. Cross-hatching and the little spiral towards the upper left are also common Tesuque embellishments. In contrast to San Ildefonso storage jars of this period (as, e.g., fig. 19), this vessel has a flat support area, which is typical of Tesuque.

42
Powhoge Polychrome (Tesuque Variety) Storage Jar

Circa 1850. H. 50 cm. School of American Research, Santa Fe, N.M., cat. no. 3990/12

Several motifs on this fine storage jar, such as the paired elements with spiral terminations, are borrowed from Zuni (see, e.g., fig. 153); the large spirals with triple triangular caps are also borrowed, in this case from Zia or Zuni. Numerous typical Tesuque features are present, including the finger-like feathers in the neck-band decoration, the rectangular areas in the black motifs, the tall key motifs, diagonally hatched strips, and the radiating feather cluster in the rectangle at the lower left (see also figs. 38 and 39).

43
Powhoge Polychrome (Tesuque Variety?) Storage Jar

Circa 1840. H. 41 cm. Coll. Mr. and Mrs. Larry Frank

This excellent storage jar appears to have been made at Tesuque, except for the underbody shape, which suggests a Cochiti origin. The paste contains crushed crystalline fragments, also a Cochiti trait. However, the slip is completely typical of Tesuque ceramics, and the decoration is characteristic of Tesuque in every respect: the wavy lines; the finger-like feathers; the pendent ovals (leaves?); the open latticework. Here, then, is a mystery. Did a Cochiti woman marry a Tesuque man? Did she construct the pot in typical Cochiti form with Cochiti materials and the husband decorate it on slip obtained from his Tesuque home?

44
Tesuque Polychrome Footed Bowl
Circa 1880. Diam. 24 cm. Coll. John Goodwin, cat. no. 20/698, no. 58

Footed bowls are characteristic of the ceremonial pottery of Tesuque Pueblo (see also fig. 45). The terraced treatment of the rim in this example indicates manufacture for sacred use. The exterior has a patina imparted by the natural oil of countless hands passing the bowl from person to person in the sacred Kiva. Prominent are the paired Avanyus (plumed serpents; here, however, lacking plumes) with lightning emitted from their mouths. The round-capped motifs pointing upwards and downwards appear to be feather symbols (see also fig. 8).

45
Footed Bowls of Tatungue Polychrome and Tesuque Polychrome
Left: Circa 1890. *Right:* Circa 1870. Diam. 14 cm. and 23 cm., respectively. Coll. Francis Harlow

These vessels illustrate two styles of footed bowls made for the sacred Indian ceremonies of Tesuque Pueblo. The wavy line on the exterior of the right-hand bowl is a typical Tesuque feature. The clustered arcs below are cloud banks, and the adjacent crisscross lines represent stars. On the interior are cloud banks supported by a triangular base, and with these are lightning symbols terminating in arrowheads and embellished with dots in their zigzag stems.

The bowl on the left illustrates typical Tatungue Polychrome features; in contrast with San Ildefonso Polychrome, the red areas are only partially edged in black. The interior shows cloud banks above a rainbow arc, with a human interpretation for the clouds, and lightning symbols terminating in arrowheads. A plumed serpent guards each side of the interior. On the exterior, rain falls in the form of vertical dashes below the cloud man. On each side is a mythical bird.

46
Tesuque Polychrome Ceremonial Bowl

Circa 1900. 24x22 cm. Coll. Mr. and Mrs. Larry Frank

This nicely made vessel has seen surprisingly little use since its manufacture about 1900. In type it is classed as polychrome because of the presence of a bright red glossy slip on the bottom of the base. In classic Tewa style, the slip has a beautiful stone-stroked finish. At the left on the exterior two plumed serpents with lightning tongues and cloud-bedecked bodies face each other over a bank of clouds (only one serpent is visible in the illustration). At the right are two sacred bears, also with lightning bolts issuing from their mouths. One bear (visible in the illustration) is standing on all four legs, while the other is sitting on his haunches. Star motifs are sprinkled about.

47

48

49

47
Tesuque Polychrome Ceremonial Bowl

Circa 1890. Diam. 36 cm. Museum of New Mexico, Santa Fe, N.M., cat. no. 7598/12

Birds, a handsome lion, and a human (not visible) decorate the surface of this round-based ceremonial bowl from Tesuque. Clouds, rain, lightning, and stylized feathers can be easily identified (see also figs. 27, 28, 45).

48 & 49
Tesuque Black-on-tan Ceremonial Bowl

Circa 1880. Diam. 35 cm. Coll. Mr. and Mrs. Larry Frank

These two views show the interior and exterior of a ceremonial bowl that would be Tesuque Polychrome except for the complete absence of red. The exterior is dominated by cloud figures, stars, arcs with appended triangles (see also fig. 8), and a damaged bird. Tesuque was virtually the only pueblo to use parallel lines with diagonal hatching for framing-line embellishment in the late nineteenth century. The wavy lines between the tall key motifs also present a thoroughly Tesuque appearance. On the interior (see fig. 49) are variants of the motifs on the exterior, as well as lightning zigzags with arrowhead terminations, multiple crisscross stars, and cornstalk (?) motifs.

50 & 51
Tesuque Polychrome Water Jar
Circa 1880. H. 27 cm. Coll. Mr. and Mrs. Larry Frank

A thoroughly typical expression of Tesuque Polychrome is exemplified by this large water jar. Wavy, thick but graceful lines, pendent teardrops, pendent arcs, tall key motifs, semicircular "pods," lacy wings, and pronged tridents, all combine to give this vessel an appearance that could not have been achieved at a place other than Tesuque. Two views are shown to illustrate the independence of the principal motifs from one another. Many of the features so well developed here can be seen in incipient form on the vessels described earlier as the Tesuque variety of Powhoge Polychrome (as in figs. 38–43).

52
Tesuque Polychrome Bowl
Circa 1880. Diam. 41 cm. Museum of New Mexico, Santa Fe, N.M., cat. no. 18784/12

Large, wide-mouthed bowls of the type shown here may have originated prior to 1800 (see also fig. 41) and continued through the nineteenth century. Typical Tesuque dimpling of the surface has resulted in a splotchy erosion pattern. Notice the circular elements on leafy stems and a Pueblo version of the swastika at the right, both diagnostic of Tesuque pottery decoration.

53
Tesuque Polychrome Water Jars
Circa 1890. H. 20 cm. and 27 cm., respectively. Coll. Mr. and Mrs. Larry Frank

Two fairly typical water jars of Tesuque Polychrome are illustrated. The one on the left resembles jars from San Ildefonso, but paste and dimpled surface appearance indicate a Tesuque origin. The neck-band decoration on the right-hand jar harks back to the early nineteenth century.

54
Tesuque Polychrome Storage Jar

Circa 1880. H. 46 cm. School of American
Research, Santa Fe, N.M., cat. no. 2809/12

The ultimate in Tesuque Polychrome exuberance
of design is well illustrated by this characteristic
big storage jar. Around the neck the motifs somewhat resembling a Greek fret and the diagonally
hatched framing lines are noteworthy. Motifs on
the body include cornstalks, tall keys, trident
caps, cross-hatching, radiant sun symbols (or
flowers?), and solid scallops with proximal
edging that are almost completely unique to
Tesuque decoration.

55
Tatungue Polychrome Bowl

Circa 1880. Diam. 29 cm. Coll. Francis Harlow

San Juan influence on the form of bowls can be observed here by comparison with figure 3. In style both vessels preserve something resembling the traditions of Tewa Polychrome (as, e.g., in fig. 7), although significantly modified. The red decorations are edged with black, a feature that suggests a relatively early date for the type. Note the omission of red from one of the elements on the left. A peculiar oversight is the absence of a red band at the top of the underbody.

56
Tatungue Polychrome Storage Jar

Circa 1890. H. 36 cm. Coll. Mr. and Mrs. John Painter

A restrained use of red on this superb storage jar occurs only with black edging, visible in the arcs of the neck band, which seems related to the Zia neck band in figure 100. The embellished diagonal midbody lines are a typical Tesuque design statement. Solid semicircles, with proximal arcs disconnected from framing lines, are characteristic of Tesuque. To these are appended motifs borrowed from Zuni, as in figure 42, as well as some that seem like little insects.

57

bowl the Cochiti slip is quite grainy and poorly polished. The paste is slightly more like that of Cochiti than typical of Tesuque, having more rock fragments than usual. The sculptured birds (one broken off) are an unusual feature, which is known to occur also on Nambe pottery. The walls are thick and heavy. The black paint is dense, and there is no red anywhere on the vessel. Typical ceremonial motifs are used, but the execution of the decoration lacks the delicacy of previous examples; see, for example, figure 45, made only a few years earlier.

58
Nambe Polychrome Storage Jar

Circa 1780. H. 31 cm. School of American Research, Santa Fe, N.M., cat. no. 4272/12

Roughly spherical in shape and red-banded at the top of the unslipped underbody, this Nambe Polychrome storage jar shares traits in common with Powhoge Polychrome of the same age. Typical also is the decoration in two bands, bounded above and below by double framing lines, but a Nambe modification is seen in the dots that embellish the vertical lines dividing each band. Mica flakes in the paste, soft slip, and careless execution of the decoration are other Nambe traits. The star-like pattern was much in favor during the early days of Nambe Polychrome and Powhoge Polychrome and occurs even to more recent times in Kiua Polychrome (as, e.g., in figs. 73 and 76).

58

59
Nambe Polychrome Storage Jar

Circa 1780. H. 42 cm. Coll. Francis Harlow

Like the jar in figure 58, this storage jar bears the dark, soft, and easily eroded slip of the Nambe variety. Notice the unusual occurrence of two narrow upper bands of decoration (a single band was usual), and the dark red band below the decoration. A holdover of the feather symbols of early eighteenth-century pottery can be seen here, each feather pair nestled in a "pod," which later becomes a common feature of Tesuque design.

57
Footed Bowl of Unnamed Tesuque Pottery

Circa 1910. Diam. 22 cm. Coll. Mr. and Mrs. Larry Frank

The occurrence of Cochiti slip on Tesuque pottery has not been recognized as a type with a separate name. On this ceremonial-style footed

60
Nambe Polychrome Water Jars
Circa 1800. H. 25 cm. and 27 cm., respectively.
Coll. Francis Harlow

Of these two water jars, the one on the left is
especially typical of Nambe Polychrome. Both
vessels show the erosion that easily removes
the relatively soft slip over many years of use.
The narrow decorative band on the upperbody
of the left-hand jar suggests the Santa Ana–
Acoma style of that period. Absence of the upper
narrow band on the right-hand jar is unusual
but not unique.

Northeast Keres Pueblos

Cochiti and Santo Domingo Pueblos (Kiua Polychrome period)

These two pueblos are the most northeastern of the Keresan language villages. They lie just to the south of the Tewa villages and accordingly have felt strong ceramic influences from those neighbors. After the Indian revolt of 1680 this influence became especially strong. Both Santo Domingo and Cochiti discontinued their manufacture of glazeware. For a while they imported pottery from the Puname (early Zia) and Tewa areas, and then gradually these pueblos began to make their own copies of the Tewa styles, using carbon paint for the Tewa-like decorations. The classic type of Tewa-like pottery at Santo Domingo and Cochiti bears the name Kiua Polychrome (see color pls. VII–IX; figs. 61–78). Kiua is the Indian name for Santo Domingo, and the type was made there principally in the period from 1760 to the present. At Cochiti also the type began about 1760 but by 1830 showed signs of evolving into a different one. By 1850 the style was so distinct that we give it the name Cochiti Polychrome (see below, Cochiti Pueblo). Nevertheless, Kiua Polychrome continues to be made even now at both Cochiti and Santo Domingo.

Many vessels of Kiua Polychrome have been made in recent years and quite a few survive, in contrast to Powhoge Polychrome, which was rarely made after about 1830. In both cases the oldest examples are usually the large storage jars, which are the least likely to be broken because of their sheltered confinement in seldom-entered storage rooms. As a result of persistent domestic use, rarely are any but the more recent smaller jars and bowls preserved.

Kiua Polychrome jars and bowls have simple utilitarian forms. Bowls are nearly hemispherical, with flat bottoms. Jars are nearly spherical, with a short neck and slightly out-turned rim. Water jars, usually about 20 to 30 centimeters tall, have a concave depression on the base to facilitate carrying the vessel on the head; larger jars are convexly rounded or slightly flattened on the base. The arrangement of the decoration is much like that of Powhoge Polychrome.

The upper part of the exterior of a jar or bowl is covered with white slip as background for the black carbon paint. The lower slopes are bare paste, usually well smoothed. At the contact line between white slip and paste occurs the red band that is such a distinctive feature of the period before about 1930; thereafter, the entire underbody is usually covered with red slip. Compared with Powhoge Polychrome, the red band is quite wide, and the red is more orange in hue, softer, and flakes more easily than the hard dark red of Powhoge Polychrome. On jars the decoration is in two bands, a narrow upper one and a wider lower one. In the upper band the motifs are simple, formal, and geometric. The lower band may be similar in style or may be somewhat more elaborate, but it is seldom as elaborate as on Powhoge Polychrome.

The earliest examples of Kiua Polychrome have red-painted rim tops; very few such vessels are preserved today. Vessels from about 1800 have black-painted rim tops, in consistent contrast to vessels of Powhoge Polychrome. Kiua and Powhoge Polychrome differ as follows:

Powhoge Polychrome	*Kiua Polychrome*
1 The paste is fine in texture, only rarely having extraneous inclusions.	The paste is relatively coarsely tempered with light-colored crystalline fragments.
2 The slip is stone polished, and crazes (crackles) finely and blindly (the cracks are not interconnected).	The slip is usually rag polished, and sometimes crazes to form scabs with upturned edges.
3 Rim tops are red.	After about 1800, rim tops are black.
4 The black paint is sometimes rather watery.	The black paint is rather often dark and dense.
5 The red band below the white slip is usually dark, thickly applied, hard, and narrow.	The red band is somewhat orange in hue, softer, more flaky, and relatively wide.

It should be stressed that, although Kiua Polychrome was originally a copy of Powhoge Polychrome, it has certainly assumed a distinctive style of its own. The many Kiua Polychrome vessels that exist show boldness and vitality, with a certain decisive strength of design that the finer, more artistic Powhoge vessels may lack. In some cases the patterns exhibit a fascinating positive-negative dual character, a particular feature of Kiua Polychrome storage jars. All have unmistakable power at a distance and ingenuity in their clear, economical statement of design. The Kiua Polychrome rag-polished slip is attractive, and in many instances rivals the beauty of the stone-polished Powhoge Polychrome.

Cochiti Pueblo

The pottery type known as Cochiti Polychrome (see color pl. X; figs. 80–88) developed out of nearly one hundred years of the Kiua Polychrome tradition. By 1850 certain definitive Cochiti characteristics were discernible, principally in design. Cochiti motifs are isolated decorations, often with little relation to one another. The lines are finer than on Kiua Polychrome, giving the motifs a lighter, fussier appearance. A typical Cochiti feature is the habit of embellishing the encircling framing lines with pendent figures, usually simple arcs or triangles, but sometimes enigmatic, complicated adaptations of older feather motifs. The old style of red banding below the decorated area persisted until about 1925 and finally gave way to the overall application of red slip to the underbodies of vessels, a practice serving as a partial means of dating.

The employment of red in the decoration was established at Cochiti by perhaps as early as 1880, although its use was quite rare and limited. Intriguing bird-shaped vessels in great variety were embellished with innovative decoration meant primarily for tourist markets. By 1890 Cochiti potters began to experiment with making human figurines, forming them in striking poses and with vivid expressions. There seemed to be a loosening of traditional disciplines, an attempt to cope with new economic growth in the Southwest by meeting it halfway. Thus sacred ceremonial symbols of clouds, rain, and lightning appeared on Cochiti vessels, together with depictions of various little creatures, cornstalks and the sacred clown, cloud persons, and animals (mountain lions, lizards, badgers, deer, turtles) freely drawn. A whole world of Pueblo religious motifs can be seen. Cochiti animal and bird figures are delightful, and their combination with nature symbols and the occasional use of red produce quite appealing pottery. To their Santo Domingo neighbors, only six miles distant, however, the secular use of these motifs is shocking. Conservative traditions in Santo Domingo have kept this pueblo from placing such sacred representations on secular vessels.

Cochiti potters are also known to have made true ceremonial vessels, some of which are very delicately decorated, others bold in pattern and form, but all having a decidedly special attraction. Unique to the Northeast Keres area are ceremonial vessels in the form of rectangular pitchers.

Following the widespread turn-of-the-century slump in pottery making, Cochiti enjoyed a renaissance that may be attributable to one particularly gifted potter whose name is unknown. In the face of declining pottery standards she turned out a number of fine vessels. Some of her jars are the largest ever made at Cochiti. In general, Cochiti vessels are both traditional and innovative and are delicately and sensitively decorated.

Santo Domingo Pueblo

When some of the potters of Santo Domingo finally began to break from the traditional styles of Kiua Polychrome, the departure was much less extreme than at Cochiti. The resulting vessels, known as Santo Domingo Polychrome (see color pl. XI; figs. 89, 90), are distinguished from Kiua Polychrome as follows:

Santo Domingo Polychrome	Kiua Polychrome
1 The jars are relatively tall.	The shapes of jars are squat and more nearly spherical.
2 Decoration on the jars is usually not broken up into panels or bands.	Jars almost always have a narrow band of decoration around the neck, and a much wider band around the body, the latter usually divided into panels by vertical lines.
3 Red is frequently used in the motifs.	No red is used in the motifs.
4 Decoration on the jars is often naturalistic, with birds and foliage usually predominant.	Decoration on the jars is usually geometric.
5 Bowls are rare, few being made.	Bowls are common and at least as numerous as jars.

The innate conservatism of the pueblo persisted, and even today Santo Domingo remains a citadel of traditionalism. In most respects, jars and bowls continue to be made much as they were in earlier times. The most apparent exception is the introduction of red into the motifs. Although red in the motifs is rare at Cochiti, it became more acceptable at Santo Domingo and is relatively often seen on pottery produced there after 1900. Excellent ceramics have been produced at Santo Domingo even today.

It is not always easy to distinguish between the more traditional styles of Santo Domingo and Cochiti pottery since the villages are close to each other in language, location, and basic traditions. The following summary gives some of the principal points of distinction:

Santo Domingo	*Cochiti*
1 Motifs are heavier and blacker, and more geometrically continuous.	Fussy, thin-line motifs, often with pendent figures (simple arcs or triangles), and variations on the feather symbols are common.
2 Vessels are almost never sculptured beyond the basic utilitarian forms.	There are human and animal figurines, bird-shaped vessels, and sculptured reptiles on the sides of vessels, in addition to simple utilitarian forms.
3 Decoration is simpler and less involved, and never incorporates sacred symbols or any animal forms other than birds on secular vessels.	Cochiti employs the sacred symbols of rain, clouds, and lightning and both animal and bird forms on secular vessels.
4 Red is commonly incorporated into Santo Domingo Polychrome after 1900.	The use of red is rare and limited in Cochiti Polychrome from around 1880.
5 Bowl interiors are seldom decorated.	Bowl interiors are often decorated.

Bowls of Kiua Polychrome are especially common at Santo Domingo, both dough bowls and the small "chili" bowls that are being made today. Not only are these for sale to tourists, they are still used quite commonly for table service and for carrying food to celebrants of ceremonial rites in the sacred Kivas. It is common to see a woman's name scratched or painted on the bottom of a bowl, the purpose being owner identification when the Kiva meal is over.

Santo Domingo vessels excel in the strong expressionistic effect they create. Their motifs are bold and usually well planned and well integrated in arrangement. The occurrence of the ceremonial break, the interruption of the encircling framing lines, is much more common on Santo Domingo and Cochiti vessels than on vessels from San Ildefonso and Tesuque.

Ceremonial pottery from Santo Domingo is rarely seen by non-Indian eyes. Its decoration is bolder than that of Cochiti, although many of the motifs (e.g., clouds and lightning) are common to both villages. Santo Domingo ceremonial vessels are occasionally square or rectangular, and the distinctive pitcher form is also seen at this pueblo.

61
Kiua Polychrome (Cochiti Variety) Storage Jar

Circa 1770. H. 38 cm. Coll. Marie Chabot

Kiua pottery is made at the two Keres pueblos of Cochiti and Santo Domingo. The red rim top indicates that this Kiua Polychrome storage jar is an early example, since after about 1800 the rim tops were painted black. The medallions resemble an earlier motif of Powhoge Polychrome (as in fig. 38), while the dark border around the right-hand medallion later became common on Tesuque Polychrome. Kiua Polychrome traits (distinguished from those of Powhoge Polychrome) can be seen in the striations on the slip from rag polishing and the ceremonial breaks in the framing lines, common to the pottery of Cochiti and Santo Domingo Polychrome but rarer on Powhoge Polychrome.

62
Kiua Polychrome (Santo Domingo Variety) Storage Jar

Circa 1790. H. 51 cm. Coll. Francis Harlow

The red rim top proves this storage jar to be an early example of Kiua Polychrome. Here the red band below the decoration is wide, whereas the red band in Powhoge Polychrome is narrow. Considerable restraint is used in the decoration, a characteristic of the positive-negative pattern often seen on Santo Domingo vessels. The narrow neck-band decoration on this vessel is quite common on early Kiua Polychrome jars.

63
Kiua Polychrome (Cochiti Variety) Storage Jar

Circa 1800. H. 70 cm. Coll. Francis Harlow

Relative delicacy and fussy femininity distinguish the Cochiti variety of Kiua Polychrome

tinguish the Cochiti variety of Kiua Polychrome from the bolder, more masculine Santo Domingo variety. A very common Cochiti feature is the unpainted (negative) leaf-like elements in the black corner fillings. Spiral motifs with proximal embellished companion lines are also frequently seen on Cochiti vessels. Triangles pendent from the framing lines are rare for Santa Domingo, common for Cochiti.

64
Kiua Polychrome (Santo Domingo Variety) Jar

Circa 1810. H. 30 cm. Coll. Francis Harlow

The bold strength of this jar, characteristic of Santo Domingo, shows especially well when compared with the somewhat similar Cochiti vessel in figure 63. The spiral volutes on the Santo Domingo jar consist of only one embellished line, in contrast to those on the Cochiti vessel.

63

64

65
Kiua Polychrome (Cochiti Variety) Storage Jar

Circa 1840. H. 50 cm. Coll. Mr. and Mrs. Larry Frank

This marvelous old storage jar combines traditional motifs with innovative patterns. The capless feathers on the spiral stems and the narrow band of decoration at the neck are traditional. The wavy lines in the medallion and the decoration within the neck are innovations. There is a self-conscious extreme in the treatment of the ceremonial break, which cleaves the pattern from top to bottom. The black rim top and wide red banding are conspicuous traits that join with the paste, tempered with crushed crystalline rock, and rag-wiped slip to contrast strongly with Powhoge Polychrome vessels of the same period.

66

Kiua Polychrome (Cochiti Variety) Jar

Circa 1850. H. 38 cm. Coll. Mr. and Mrs.
Bernard Lopez

The ultimate in beautiful mellow tan patina can
be seen on this jar. The decoration presents
another variant of the motif seen in figures 63,
64, and 65. Unusual features are the short neck
and the use of single framing lines at all levels,
rather than the usual paired lines. Two bands
of decoration at the neck also represent something of an innovation.

67

**Kiua Polychrome (Cochiti Variety?)
Storage Jar**

Circa 1870. H. 47 cm. Coll. Mr. and Mrs.
Larry Frank

Several features confuse the classification of this
vessel: the watermelon shape; the multiple framing lines at the shoulder; the multiple panel lines;
the extreme enlargement of the corner-filling
motifs. Characteristic features of Kiua Polychrome
are present in the form of the underbody, the
wide red banding, the striated rag-wiped slip,
and the black rim top. Such traditional elements
as the double terminations of the capless feathers are also retained in the decoration. The dual
positive-negative treatment of the decoration is
clearly evident.

68

**Kiua Polychrome (Cochiti Variety)
Storage Jar**

Circa 1870. H. 51 cm. Coll. Mr. and Mrs.
Larry Frank

Perhaps the most interesting feature of this storage jar is the nature of the ceremonial break. In
contrast to the treatment given it on the storage
jar in figure 65, here the top-to-bottom cleavage
is rendered relatively inconspicuous. Note the
attractive "Maltese Cross" motif, with the Cochiti
negative leaf pattern within the positive black
areas.

69

69
Kiua Polychrome (Cochiti Variety) Storage Jar

Circa 1850. H. 39 cm. Coll. Mr. and Mrs. Larry Frank

Simplicity and restraint characterize the storage jar seen here and the one in figure 70. Both vessels lack the usual narrow neck band; but the storage jar shown here has a single pair of panel lines as a device to emphasize the ceremonial break. The decorative motif is clearly reminiscent of the Powhoge Polychrome motif seen in figure 17.

70

70
Kiua Polychrome (Cochiti Variety) Storage Jar

Circa 1880. H. 41 cm. Coll. Mr. and Mrs. Larry Frank

The medallion motif appears to have persisted for a longer time on Kiua Polychrome than on Powhoge Polychrome. Absence of a narrow decorative neck band is unusual, but the triple upper framing lines especially are innovative. Inconspicuous line breaks are visible in all the framing lines.

71
Kiua Polychrome (Cochiti Variety) Dough Bowl

Circa 1860. Diam. 46 cm. Coll. Mr. and Mrs. Larry Frank

The strongly flexured form of this bowl is somewhat extreme for Kiua Polychrome; compare its profile with those of figures 72–75. An apparent sloppiness in painting the solid black areas turns out, on closer inspection, to be in actuality an intentional incorporation of narrow unpainted crescents. The practice of binding the vessel to prevent further cracking is traditional.

72
Kiua Polychrome (Cochiti Variety) Dough Bowl

Circa 1860. Diam. 46 cm. Coll. Mr. and Mrs. Larry Frank

The Cochiti variety of Kiua Polychrome is more intricate and less massively blunt and bold than the vessels from Santo Domingo, as this bowl indicates. Here the star motif has been incorporated into the decoration, with various differences from the examples in figures 22, 23, 24, and 60 (left). An oversight in the decoration, visible where the left-hand tip of the repeat on the extreme right is not filled with black, leaves the design subtly incomplete. A large bowl like this would hold several days' supply of dough for a Pueblo family.

73

74

73
Kiua Polychrome (Santo Domingo Variety) Dough Bowl

Circa 1860. Diam. 42 cm. Coll. Mr. and Mrs. Larry Frank

This vessel illustrates the finest expression of Kiua Polychrome in bowls from Santo Domingo. The style of decoration is traditional, derived from Powhoge Polychrome (see figs. 14 and 19). Other features—the typical wide red banding, rag-polished slip, and black rim top—combine to show at once that this is not a Tewa product.

74
Kiua Polychrome (Cochiti Variety?) Dough Bowl

Circa 1900. Diam. 48 cm. Coll. Mr. and Mrs. Larry Frank

Narrow framing lines and delicacy combine to suggest a Cochiti origin for this Kiua Polychrome dough bowl. The absence of planning in the decoration resulted in the amusing compression of the pattern in the area of the ceremonial break. Omission of interior decoration is typical of bowls of Kiua Polychrome.

75
Kiua Polychrome (Santo Domingo Variety) Bowl

Circa 1915. Diam. 28 cm. Coll. Mr. and Mrs. Larry Frank

The bold decoration on this late example of Kiua Polychrome suggests a Santo Domingo

origin. Such bowls are made to the present day, although this one is more than several decades old. The panel on the right is dropped in placement and the circle it bears is more completely round than the others, thus breaking the monotony of the design.

76
Kiua Polychrome (Cochiti Variety) Jar

Circa 1830. H. 20 cm. Museum of New Mexico, Santa Fe, N.M., cat. no. 12268/12

Most of our illustrations of Kiua Polychrome are of large storage jars or relatively recent bowls, because small jars like this one have only rarely survived to the present. In style the decoration is essentially that of figure 73, modified by curves to a slightly more graceful appearance. A Cochiti origin is indicated by the motifs pendent from the upper framing lines.

77
Kiua Polychrome Jar

Circa 1860. H. 18 cm. Coll. Mr. and Mrs. Larry Frank

This little jar, as rare as the one in figure 76, is so unusual as to make the pueblo of origin impossible to identify. Not only the decoration itself but the single framing lines suggest a significant break from the usual traditions of Kiua Polychrome. Enough traditional features (paste, slip, form) are present, however, to indicate a Kiua Polychrome classification.

75

76

77

78
Kiua Polychrome
(Santo Domingo Variety) Pitcher

Circa 1920. H. 12 cm. Coll. Mr. and Mrs. Larry Frank

This oblong, subquadrate pitcher is a variant of the sacred ceremonial pottery made at Santo Domingo and Cochiti after about 1850 (see, e.g., fig. 87). This example represents Kiua Polychrome at its finest: light in weight, beautifully slipped and polished, exquisitely painted with traditional motifs, and well fired. The interior is unpainted except for a row of dots near the rim, visible on the far side.

79
Kiua Black-on-red Storage Jar

Circa 1880. H. 41 cm. Coll. Mr. and Mrs. Larry Frank

The rare old vessels of Kiua Black-on-red that have been preserved may all have been made at Cochiti Pueblo. The surface color of the decorated area varies from a shade of pink (as on this storage jar) to a dark rust red. Otherwise the type is identical with Kiua Polychrome.

80
Cochiti Polychrome Storage Jar

Circa 1840. H. 39 cm. Coll. Mr. and Mrs.
Larry Frank

Isolation of the motifs, absence of panel lines,
and inclusion of naturalistic figures, all combine
to identify this storage jar as Cochiti Polychrome.
It is conservative enough in its other features so
that, were the bird figure not present, we would
call this Kiua Polychrome, Cochiti variety. Noteworthy characteristics in this example are: extreme heaviness (an invisible trait); entire absence
of lower framing lines; the black rim top; the
presence of ceremonial breaks in the medallion
itself. The dot-filled leaves within the medallion
occur quite frequently on Cochiti vessels in the
period before about 1850.

81
Cochiti Polychrome Storage Jar

Circa 1880. H. 37 cm. Coll. Mr. and Mrs.
Larry Frank

This jar is a later version of the Cochiti jar with
a bird motif shown in figure 80. Although the
later birds are primitive, the overall design is
much more delicate, complex, and busy. The tree
to the left is very bushy and full of leaves compared to the other two trees. Even the roots of
the trees are indicated. Two sets of birds, in the
top and middle zones, decorate the jar. Trees
and birds completely fill the compartments in
the design, with wavy dot-filled lines occupy-
ing the bottom of the band of decoration, which
is interrupted by a ceremonial break.

82
Cochiti Polychrome Storage Jar
Circa 1850. H. 49 cm. Coll. Mr. and Mrs.
Larry Frank

This large, handsome Cochiti storage jar includes in its decoration pronghorn antelopes supporting eagles (top) and other animal life, suggesting that the jar was made for a special ceremonial purpose. Notice the dots present in some of the circular areas. A bald eagle (invisible to the viewer) is painted in the top band opposite the antelopes. Even though storage jars fared better in the back rooms of pueblos than other vessels, it is a wonder that such a large jar as this one survived to the present day.

83 & 84
Cochiti Polychrome Dough Bowl

Circa 1900. Diam. 43 cm. Museum of New Mexico, Santa Fe, N.M., cat. no. 41805/12

Both the exterior and the interior of this excellent bowl are shown to illustrate the difference between the traditional Kiua Polychrome style (the exterior) and the more free and informal Cochiti Polychrome style (the interior). The ex-terior design harks back to the older Powhoge Polychrome styles of figures 14, 19, 22, 23, and 24, with traditional banding below the area of decoration. On the interior the innovative bird motif breaks away from the traditional bird in figure 80, and shows considerable evolution in rendering. Some traditional traits are retained, like the feather symbols and negative leaf patterns (as also in figs. 13 and 63).

85
Cochiti Polychrome Jar
Circa 1920. H. 18 cm. Museum of New Mexico, Santa Fe, N.M., cat. no. 12267/12

This small jar is significant because it is a secular vessel bearing many ceremonial symbols. Use of these sacred motifs on any but the most secret ceremonial vessels was at one time forbidden, but Cochiti Pueblo began to use them shortly before 1900, a shocking act to the more conservative nearby pueblos. Employment of disconnected motifs, both secular and sacred, is typical of Cochiti. Traditional features include the black rim top, formal decoration in the narrow neck band, double framing lines at the shoulder, solid arcs pendent from the framing line, and typical Cochiti rag-polished slip. Absent are the usual lower framing lines, red banding, and unslipped underbody.

86
Cochiti Polychrome Storage Jar
Circa 1915. H. 45 cm. Coll. Mr. and Mrs. Larry Frank

The short neck and the replacement of the lowermost framing lines by a series of double arcs are somewhat unusual for this large, heavy Cochiti Polychrome storage jar. Corner-filling motifs in the upper band have unpainted (negative) leaf motifs in a style almost identical to the earlier pattern in figures 63 and 65. The well-executed upper band of decoration may have been painted by a different artist from the painter of the intriguing animals and the arcs below.

87
Cochiti Polychrome Ceremonial Rectangular Pitcher
Circa 1880. H. 14 cm. Coll. Francis Harlow

Although Cochiti potters often painted sacred symbols on secular vessels, this rectangular pitcher is an example of true ceremonial pottery. In form the little pitcher is unique to the ceremonial (and recently to the secular) pottery of the Northeast Keres pueblos of Santo Domingo and Cochiti. A pottery arc that extended over the spout, similar to the structure on the left-hand

vessel in figure 45, was broken from this vessel.
The black rim top is sculptured into ceremonial
stairsteps. Among the decorative motifs are
mythical water creatures, cornstalks with ears of
corn, wavy arrows representing lightning or
serpents or both, and a checkered split structure.

88
Cochiti Polychrome
Bird-Spout Jar

Circa 1905. H. 15 cm. Coll. Mr. and Mrs.
Larry Frank

Stylistically this Cochiti Polychrome bird-spout
jar shows an extremely strong influence from
Tesuque's Tatungue Polychrome, especially in
the presence of red in the decoration and in the
embellishment of the lines. The presence of red
in the decoration is unusual for Cochiti. Cochiti
traits are the crushed crystalline paste and the
rag-polished slip. Ceremonial breaks, present
here, are almost never seen on Tesuque pottery.
On top of the handle is a motif going back to
much earlier days (as, e.g., in fig. 62).

89
Santo Domingo Polychrome
Storage Jar

Circa 1890. H. 45 cm. Coll. Mr. and Mrs.
Larry Frank

Typical features of Santo Domingo Polychrome
exhibited by this well-used storage jar are the
absence of paneling, the omission of a narrow
band of decoration on the upperbody, and the

presence of red in the motifs. One usual feature, however, is lacking—relatively tall form. The parrot represented here with an ornamented arc over the head has been borrowed from Laguna and Acoma and translated into a crude approximation of the original (see also fig. 134). The double rainbow arch also is a borrowed feature, in this case from Zia. The bold geometric decoration on the right is more typical of Santo Domingo design.

90
Santo Domingo Polychrome Storage Jar

Circa 1900. H. 50 cm. Coll. Harvey Mudd

Intrigue and mystery are suggested by the stubby, masked birds on this vessel. As on the jar in figure 89, the motif is a modified version of the parrot of Acoma and Laguna. The large flowers are quite common on Santo Domingo Polychrome vessels.

Puname Pueblos

Zia Pueblo

Zia Pueblo, in north-central New Mexico, has maintained its tradition as a leader in the production of excellent ceramics, continuing the finest of the time-honored features in a sequence of styles that show virtually no European influence and little curio-market degeneracy. Even in recent years the traditional techniques have been followed with unrelenting precision. For six centuries Zia traditions have required that ceramic clay be mixed with finely crushed black basaltic lava, a unique and distinctive feature that permits sure recognition of the pottery from this pueblo, but one that has required countless hours of backbreaking labor over the grinding stones.

Matte-paint styles of Pueblo pottery decoration originated late in the seventeenth century, replacing an earlier glaze-ware tradition. The first type (see color pl. XII; figs. 91–95) is known as Puname Polychrome (1680–1740), a name derived from the designation for the "people of the west," while its descendant (see figs. 96 and 97), San Pablo Polychrome (1740–1800), bears an old Spanish name for the pueblo of Zia. As at most other pueblos during this period the designers of pottery were much preoccupied with the feather symbol. At Zia especially, this sacred motif was painted on almost every surviving eighteenth-century vessel in various modifications. Until about 1765 all these vessels were endowed with one feature that is particularly useful for dating purposes: The rim top was always painted red. After that date, during the last three decades of San Pablo Polychrome and thereafter, the rim tops of Zia vessels have always been painted black.

bird" volute, executed in a diagonal, double-ended shape that is both graceful and efficient in its use of the available space. Following the usual prescription of the period, the decorations were arranged in two bands, the volutes in the wider band on the body, and a simpler pattern in a narrower band around the neck. As at the Tewa villages, a red band separated the cream-colored slip from the unslipped underbody. Trios Polychrome jars are distinguished from San Palbo Polychrome by the presence of a decorated neck and by the treatment of the motifs. In design layout the water jars of Trios Polychrome ignore the old formality of a four-panel arrangement.

Around 1850 Zia Polychrome began to replace Trios Polychrome, completing the transition by 1870, and persisting to the present (see color pls. XV and XVI; figs. 105–110). Several features serve to differentiate water jars of Trios Polychrome from those of Zia Polychrome:

Trios Polychrome	*Zia Polychrome*
1 The volute motif is relatively bold and crude in execution.	The volute motif, when present, is much neater and more elaborate.
2 The jars have round underslopes that curve gently into the concave base that facilitates carrying the vessel on the head.	Zia Polychrome jars have a straighter underbody with an angular incurve at the base.
3 The jars are globular, with the greatest diameter placed at about half-height.	The greatest diameter is placed quite high, well above half-height.
4 The bare paste of the underbody below the red band is rougher and less glossy.	The bare paste of the underbody below the red band is much better polished, so that the red band may be difficult to distinguish from the burnished brownish-red surface of the paste.

Puname Polychrome	*San Pablo Polychrome*
1 The vessels have a red rim top.	The rim top changed in color from red to black in 1765.
2 The decorative area is divided into relatively equal panels.	The vessels have two wide panels and two narrow panels, or occasionally three of each.
3 The jars have a markedly undercut underbody (flaring outward), a midbody bulge, and a straighter insloping upperbody with no neck. Bowls are similar in shape to those of Tewa Polychrome.	The jars have nearly spherical shapes with very short necks that lack decoration.
4 The jars usually have a band of red arc motifs below the main decorated area.	The jars have red arc motifs up to about 1760, but none thereafter.
5 The feather symbols are more recognizable, often showing the paired split-feather variation.	The feather symbols are more stylized.

Puname Polychrome and San Pablo Polychrome are to Zia Pueblo what Tewa Polychrome and Ogapoge Polychrome are to San Ildefonso and Tesuque, in that those ceramics attained heights of excellence that were never again quite equaled.

The nineteenth century opened for Zia Pueblo with the development of a new pottery style known as Trios Polychrome (see color pls. XIII and XIV; figs. 98–106), a designation based on an older version of the village name. Especially notable was the production of numerous huge storage jars and many water jars. Large numbers of the latter were constructed with an astonishing degree of similarity to one another. The motifs are almost universally variants of the "rain-

The large dough-mixing bowls of Trios Polychrome are also quite distinctive. Like large bowls from Zuni, another conservative pueblo, they show more traditionalism and less innovation in decoration than do the water jars. The big dough bowls perpetuate several decorative features that otherwise are characteristic only of the earlier San Pablo Polychrome.

1 There is a division of the decorative band into four panels, two wide and two narrow.
2 The wide-panel decoration includes a "double-ended" key motif from San Pablo Polychrome days that seems never to have been painted on water jars of Trios Polychrome.

In the period 1800–1870, a time when many remarkable vessels were produced, both Trios Polychrome and early Zia Polychrome were being made. Some of the Trios Polychrome jars have a slightly askew, not quite sophisticated look, with relatively unsmooth, thick slip and slightly awry, simplified decoration. This primitive charm contrasts with the all-around perfection usually found in Zia Polychrome.

Zia Polychrome jars of the early period (1850–1890) are especially attractive. They were often painted with black mineral pigment that is thick enough to impart a slightly raised texture to the decoration, a technique that is especially effective in the elaborate crosshatched geometric patterns occasionally executed during this period. (After about 1900 the black paint became flatter, grainier, and slightly browner in hue.) Great care was exercised to achieve thin and light vessels that are well formed, decorated, and finished. Characteristic of this period is a much greater freedom of decorative style, notable for the graceful use of new floral, animal (deer with antlers), and bird motifs (the typical "Zia" bird), a vigorous mode that long continued. Throughout the early 1900s large, handsome Zia Polychrome storage jars were manufactured, and a few are still made now. In the 1920s, an interesting use of orange was introduced for the background slip on the decorative area. Few examples of this practice survive, although it is occasionally used even today. As at other pueblos during this period, red banding for the underbody was abandoned about 1925 in favor of overall red slip.

Especially noteworthy are Zia ceremonial vessels with bands of arcs representing clouds, each with a face. Triangular eyes in representations of the human face are a Zia feature that apparently occurs elsewhere only at Santa Ana and Tesuque pueblos. In contrast to the degeneracy of representations of the plumed serpent on late ceremonial bowls at San Ildefonso, the Zia serpents retain the more lifelike features and meticulous rendering that are typical of the Tewa pueblos in the eighteenth century. The Zia sacred sun symbol has become one of the most famous of all Pueblo Indian motifs, having been adopted as the central figure on the New Mexico state flag. Ceremonial bowls and jars from Zia are exceptionally rare.

Santa Ana Pueblo

The divergence of Santa Ana vessels from the pottery of Zia was not apparent until after about 1720 when Ranchitos Polychrome became the first type to have unmistakable Santa Ana characteristics (see color pl. XVII; figs. 111–113). The type often resembles San Pablo Polychrome from neighboring Zia, some of the jars having very short necks that are not decorated and bearing similar motifs on the midbody. Apparently, however, Ranchitos Polychrome never has isolated red arcs in the decoration as at Zia. The transition from red to black rim tops occurred about 1765, a conclusion that is based on evidence from sherds at Las Huertas. Only one whole jar and one whole bowl with red rim tops are known to have survived to the present day. The trait that uniquely distinguishes all Santa Ana pottery from Zia pottery is the paste, and that is the most striking departure from Zia types. Santa Ana potters discovered that fine river sand is an excellent substitute for the crushed basaltic rock used at Zia to temper the clay, and it is a vastly easier material to prepare.

By about 1790, the style of Santa Ana decoration began to depart so strongly from that of Zia that recognition is usually easy even when the paste is not clearly visible. Especially characteristic are massive areas of red in the decoration, embellished by the inclusion of negative elements. These last are unpainted areas within the red, usually in the shape of crescents or semicircles. The negative areas are not edged with black at the juncture of red and white. A very similar style of decoration was employed briefly at Acoma and Laguna around 1800, but did not persist as at Santa Ana.

By the time this mode was established at Santa Ana, the potters were also decorating the necks of jars in crude imitation of Trios Polychrome, and the style (figs. 114–116) is known as Santa Ana Polychrome (1800–1940). Many Santa Ana vessels of the nineteenth century are decorated with a variant of the "Eiffel Tower" motif, and this has become a characteristic Santa Ana feature. Slowly degenerating in quality, Santa Ana's fine soft tan slip gave way to a coarse, harsh, white material, and decoration became progressively cruder until around 1940, when the decline in output amounted to virtual abandonment of the craft.

Santa Ana Polychrome has always been a relatively crudely formed and decorated type of pottery. Nevertheless, at its best there is a fresh clarity of design, a striking boldness that is quite pleasing, and a marked departure from some of the busier Pueblo styles. Also, the finest Santa Ana slip is warm in tone and attractive in appearance. At present only one Santa Ana potter continues with pottery making, employing previously popular styles.

91
Puname Polychrome Jar

Circa 1680. H. 30 cm. School of American
Research, Santa Fe, N.M., cat. no. 4312/12

This old jar has the distinction of being probably the earliest known example of matte-paint
pottery from Zia Pueblo. Close similarity in
form to Rio Grande glazed jars of the late seventeenth century, absence of red banding, and the
strongly embellished and fat descending feathers
are features that suggest an early date. In form
this jar is also close to that of Sakona Polychrome
(as, e.g., in fig. 4), although less graceful. Crushed
black basalt in the thin, hard walls proves a Zia
origin.

92
Puname Polychrome Jar

Circa 1700. H. 24 cm. School of American Research, Santa Fe, N.M., cat. no. 3161/11

The black-edged red band around the top of this
jar is a holdover from the late glaze-ware pottery of Zia, and occurs frequently on early Puname
Polychrome. In decoration the jar is similar to
two other vessels: one of Ranchitos Polychrome
(fig. 112) and one of Ashiwi Polychrome (fig.
142). Notice the triangular motif that is related
to the Ashiwi design. Sloppy filling of red areas,
so that they miss the black edging in some places,
is a frequent feature of Puname Polychrome. In
San Pablo Polychrome, which follows the period
of Puname Polychrome at Zia, the gaps between
red and black seem more intentional (see figs.
96 and 97). The absence of lower framing lines
is an indication of an early date for Puname Polychrome (as in fig. 91). Red banding appears at
the top of the unslipped underbody.

103

93
Puname Polychrome Jar

Circa 1720. H. 28 cm. University of Colorado Museum, Boulder, Colo., cat. no. 382

Puname Polychrome and Ashiwi Polychrome jars, which were produced during the same period, are very much alike in both form and decoration.

The principal differences are the presence of red arcs and a red-banded underbody on Puname Polychrome. Notice the red filling between pairs of framing lines, the black-capped feathers piled together in threes, and the black crosses in the top band like those in figure 94. This jar has a red rim top like all other vessels from Zia before about 1765.

94
Puname Polychrome Bowl

Circa 1730. Diam. 39 cm. University of Colorado Museum, Boulder, Colo., cat. no. 384

With a shape much like that of Tewa Polychrome (see figs. 6 and 7) and a style of decoration replete with early eighteenth-century feather symbols, this bowl has an early eighteenth-century date. The commonly occurring red arc has here been moved to the interior, but the only rather unusual feature of the decoration is the detachment of some of the interior motifs from the framing lines. Red filling between pairs of framing lines is a common device in Puname Polychrome, and occurs here in two places.

95
Puname Polychrome Jar

Circa 1750. H. 25 cm. School of American Research, Santa Fe, N.M., cat. no. 7887/12

This Puname Polychrome jar is completely typical in overall form, in the red arcs of the midbody band, and in the abundant use of feather sym-bols in the decoration. The caps are completely detached from the feathers, but connected to one another with a black line, a style that is especially typical of Zia pottery, even in modern times (see fig. 108). The rim top is painted red, which is typical for Zia pottery prior to about 1765.

96
San Pablo Polychrome Storage Jar

Circa 1750. H. 41 cm. Coll. Francis Harlow

This is the earliest known storage jar from Zia Pueblo. The red rim top indicates a date before 1765. The almost perfectly spherical shape, the short neck, and the arrangement of the decoration in two wide and two narrow panels are the diagnostic features of San Pablo Polychrome. The jar has a midbody band of red arcs derived from Puname Polychrome (as in figs. 93 and 97). The top of the underbody is banded in red. In the wide panels of decoration are triangular-capped feathers with a hanging feather cap attached, key motifs, and rectangular "eyes." The red device in the narrow panel on the right persists in somewhat later storage jars from Zia.

97

San Pablo Polychrome Jar

Circa 1750. H. 30 cm. School of American
Research, Santa Fe, N.M., cat. no. 3444/12

The red rim top, red arcs, and red-banded underbody are all signs of early San Pablo Polychrome jars. As in figure 96, the decorative motifs
are placed in two wide and two narrow panels,
the wide ones containing diagonal lines which
are actually, in this case, red bands. Feather, key,
and "eye" motifs are used. The key termination
of the figure at the left of center is a motif that
continues in later Zia dough bowls (as, e.g., in
fig. 102).

98

Trios Polychrome Storage Jar

Circa 1800. H. 44 cm. Museum of New Mexico,
Santa Fe, N.M., cat. no. 7716/12

This very early Trios Polychrome storage jar
shows evolution from the San Pablo Polychrome
jar in figure 96. The taller structure, the more
distinct and flaring neck, the black rim top, and
the separate band of decoration around the neck
indicate a significant change of style. By this
time the midbody band of red arcs has dis-
appeared. Although the motifs and their arrangement are similar to those of San Pablo Polychrome, two new elements are now added: the
large spiral volutes that become a "trademark"
for Trios Polychrome, and, at the far left, the
hatched figure that comes from the influence
of Kiapkwa Polychrome, a Zuni product of the
time.

99
Trios Polychrome Water Jar
Circa 1800. H. 27 cm. Coll. Francis Harlow

This Trios Polychrome water jar retains a remnant of the old four-panel arrangement. The narrow panel is represented by the C-shaped motif at the left, and the wide panel by the diagonal motif on the right, terminated at each end by a spiral volute, as in figures 100 and 103. Part of the red design is not black-edged and contains unpainted arcs in a style suggesting Santa Ana pottery of the period. Crushed black volcanic rock in the paste proves a Zia origin.

100
Trios Polychrome Jar
Circa 1820. H. 25 cm. Coll. Francis Harlow

This Trios Polychrome jar has evolved far away from San Pablo Polychrome and shares some traits with the forthcoming style, Zia Polychrome. Trios Polychrome traits are the areas of unedged red, the teardrop-shaped unpainted areas with painted teardrop fillings, and the little bird's head at the lower center. The jar differs from the later Zia Polychrome in its roughly smoothed underbody and strongly convex profile near the base, which contrasts sharply with the straight or even concave underbody profiles in figures 107 and 108.

101
Trios Polychrome Jar

Circa 1810. H. 25 cm. Coll. Francis Harlow

This fine old jar of Trios Polychrome exhibits the convexly rounded underbody, low position of the maximum diameter, and unedged red areas that characterize this type. The blunt "fingers" (at the left) and unpainted semicircular arcs and ovals are also frequently seen during this period.

102
Trios Polychrome Dough Bowl

Circa 1820. Diam. 49 cm. Coll. Mr. and Mrs. Larry Frank

This magnificent Trios Polychrome dough bowl is one of the finest surviving examples of a style that was made in abundance, with almost no change in design from about 1800 until almost the present. The sculptured shape represents a holdover from the days of Puname Polychrome (as, e.g., in fig. 94) and Tewa Polychrome (as, e.g., in fig. 7). Also descendent from earlier Zia traditions are the red key motif with a rectangular "eye," like the similar motif in figure 97, and the placement of the decoration in two narrow and two wide panels. Even a modified version of the old split-feather motif can be seen on the right (see also fig. 97).

103
Trios Polychrome Water Jar

Circa 1860. H. 26 cm. Coll. Mr. and Mrs.
Larry Frank

The evolutionary trends in Trios Polychrome
are well shown in this fine late example of the
type. At this stage, the underbody is better
smoothed, the slip is harder and whiter, and the
decoration is more precisely executed than before. There is considerable similarity in style to
the jar in figure 100, and indeed this overall
pattern has been painted on Zia vessels until recent times. By 1860 the massive red areas have
been considerably reduced and only a small part
lacks black edging.

104
Trios Polychrome Water Jar

Circa 1850. H. 25 cm. Coll. Mr. and Mrs. Larry Frank

The form of this little water jar is entirely typical for Trios Polychrome, with convexly rounded underbody, low placement of the maximum diameter, and even the tall neck (see also fig. 101). In style the decoration is in transition to the naturalistic foliage and birds of the later Zia Polychrome. An attractive feature is the very thick mineral paint used for the black lines and decorated areas, giving a relief texture that is reminiscent of the Prehistoric glaze paints. Not visible is the unusual feature that the birds face in opposing directions, some to the left and some to the right. Another feature heralding Zia Polychrome is the multiple zigzag pattern in the neck-band decoration.

105
Trios Polychrome–Zia Polychrome Transitional Storage Jar

Circa 1870. H. 30 cm. Museum of New Mexico, Santa Fe, N.M., cat. no. 30170/12

Except for a form like that of Trios Polychrome, this small storage jar is transitional between Trios and Zia Polychrome, not typical of either. It differs from typical Trios Polychrome in regard to the bird motif, which is less geometrically styled, being more naturalistic and having a rounded outline. The band of decoration on the upper-body is omitted.

106
Trios Polychrome–Zia Polychrome (Transitional) Water Jar

Circa 1870. H. 29 cm. Coll. Mr. and Mrs. Larry Frank

This attractive transitional water jar shares in common most of the features of figure 105. Zia, like its neighboring pueblos, was undergoing a new awakening to freedom from tradition, which later would materialize in progressively greater diversity and innovation in pottery styles.

107
Zia Polychrome Water Jar

Circa 1890. H. 24 cm. Coll. Francis Harlow

This Zia Polychrome water jar contrasts in form with Trios Polychrome examples, as indicated by the slightly concave underbody, the high position of the maximum diameter (forming a shoulder), the shorter neck, the profusion of painted motifs, and the harder and whiter slip. Notice the Pueblo version of the swastika.

108
Zia Polychrome Jar

Circa 1880. H. 26 cm. Museum of New Mexico, Santa Fe, N.M., cat. no. 24838/12

The concave underbody profile makes this vessel definitely an example of Zia Polychrome, although the rest of its form—for example, the tall neck and the low placement of the maximum diameter—is very reminiscent of Trios Polychrome. The feather symbols in the decoration are much like those on the Puname Polychrome jar in figure 95, especially the upper bank of feathers. The lower bank of feathers is based on the traditional device of split feathers, as in figures 97 and 141. Note that both styles of feathers also occur on the Ako Polychrome bowl in figure 121. An unusual feature is the use of yellowish pigment in place of red to fill the areas of decoration. Possibly the jar was made much later than 1880, perhaps between 1920 and 1940.

109
Zia Polychrome Jar

Circa 1900. H. 19 cm. Coll. Mr. and Mrs. Larry Frank

The naturalistic style of Zia Polychrome is represented here. The form is reminiscent of Ako Polychrome (as in fig. 120), but the similarity is coincidental. It is more likely that the form is influenced by Prehistoric seed-jar shapes, which have a strongly incurved upperbody, but usually no lip. In the early 1900s Zia deer styles evolved from this rather simple figure to more elaborate ones (see color pl. XVI). The late Zia form of the old feather symbol is seen dangling from the shoulder framing lines.

110
Zia Polychrome Water Jar

Circa 1880. H. 24 cm. Coll. Mr. and Mrs. Larry Frank

The overall geometric pattern of split leaves on this Zia Polychrome water jar is well unified and pleasing. No single element of the decoration dominates. The innate Indian feeling for design combines a certain sophistication with charming simplicity. See also figure 128.

111
Ranchitos Polychrome Jar

Circa 1750. H. 33 cm. School of American Research, Santa Fe, N.M., cat. no. 2773/12

This is the earliest known complete jar of matte-paint pottery from Santa Ana, and the only known example with a red rim top. The form strongly resembles that of the Laguna variety of Acomita Polychrome (as, e.g., in fig. 122). Origin

in Santa Ana is indicated by the paste, orangy red in color and abundantly tempered with fine, water-worn sand. In distinction from Santa Ana Polychrome jars are the undecorated neck, the red rim top, and the nature of the decoration. Unedged red areas occur at both Santa Ana and Zia during the eighteenth century. The absence of lower framing lines is noteworthy and may occur at Santa Ana only before about 1780.

112
Ranchitos Polychrome Bowl
Circa 1760. Diam. 41 cm. Coll. Francis Harlow

Like the jar in figure 111, this vessel has the unique distinction of being the only known decorated bowl of Ranchitos Polychrome with a red rim top. The simple design suggests a close relationship to the Puname Polychrome jar in figure 92. A ceremonial break is visible at the far left, and a red band encircles the top of the underbody. In form, this vessel shows strong similarity to late Pojoaque Polychrome and early Powhoge Polychrome bowls (as, e.g., in figs. 12 and 21). The interior is reddish tan in color, well smoothed and unpainted.

113
Ranchitos Polychrome Jar
Circa 1790. H. 22 cm. School of American Research, Santa Fe, N.M., cat. no. 4310/12

A nearly spherical form characterizes this compact little jar of Ranchitos Polychrome, which differs from Santa Ana Polychrome in the short, undecorated neck. It can be distinguished from late San Pablo Polychrome only by the absence of crushed volcanic rock from the paste. The unedged red motif on the right is especially characteristic of early Zia and Santa Ana matte-paint pottery (as, e.g., in fig. 114). Notice the two spiral volutes, motifs that originated perhaps as early as 1750 and became very popular around 1790. The rim top is black, and a prominent red band encircles the top of the underbody.

114
Santa Ana Polychrome Jar
Circa 1800. H. 28 cm. Coll. Francis Harlow

The style of decoration on this jar evolved directly from that in figure 111, and this example would be called Ranchitos Polychrome except for the presence of ornament on the neck. Massive areas of unedged red include the entire central part of the design, the broad stripes in the cusped arcs on the right, and the red band around the top of the underbody.

114

115
Santa Ana Polychrome Water Jar
Circa 1830. H. 25 cm. School of American
Research, Santa Fe, N.M., cat. no. 2479/12

Especially characteristic of Santa Ana Polychrome
are the massive areas of unedged red, the treatment of the upper band of decoration, and the
swinging pendulum effect in motifs left and right.
The unedged white arcs in the central red area
are traits of Acomita Polychrome. This water jar's
decoration is more dynamic than is usual for
this type.

116
Santa Ana Polychrome Jar
1830–1860. H. 26 cm. Museum of New Mexico,
Santa Fe, N.M., cat. no. 24833/12

The only atypical feature of this Santa Ana Polychrome jar is the black edging of all parts of the
red decoration. Especially characteristic are the
open areas in the massive red structures and the
"Eiffel Tower" motif just to the right of center.
The black rim top and prominent red band on
the underbody are common traits.

Other Pottery-making Pueblos

Jemez, San Felipe, Sandia, Isleta Pueblos

These four pueblos are considered together because their common bond is a lack of traditional painted pottery after about 1700. From then on, both Jemez and San Felipe made rather coarse utility ware, polished black on vessel interiors and rough on the exteriors. San Felipe potters have also produced serviceable polished red vessels, with clay and temper appearance essentially the same as those of Santa Ana and Isleta. The end of decorated pottery making in traditional styles for both of these pueblos resulted in the reliance of Jemez on imported ceramics, mainly from nearby Zia Pueblo, and the reliance of San Felipe on pottery from Zia and Cochiti. Interestingly, some of the finest eighteenth-century Zia vessels have actually been found at Jemez.

Prior to about 1700, Jemez potters manufactured a style known as Jemez Black-on-white (see fig. 117), an attractive anachronism reminiscent of the Prehistoric black-on-white styles produced at Mesa Verde centuries earlier. Jemez Black-on-white vessels are not closely related to those of other pueblos and are very rarely encountered today. Ceremonial bowls with sculptured frogs on their sides, however, are quite similar to the frog vessels that were made at Zuni.

Just at the end of the period of Jemez Black-on-white, many refugees from both Jemez and Zia moved north to Gobernador Canyon to join their comrades from Zuni and the Tewa pueblos. These Pueblo Indians had come to detest the Spanish so strongly that they were willing to join forces with their old enemies, the Navajo, who had previously been living in the Gobernador area. From this melting pot of Indian cultures, there arose a new pottery style known as Gobernador Polychrome (see fig. 118). In decoration the new type reflects the strong influence of Jemez Black-on-white; in form and arrangement of the motifs also much influence from Tewa, Northeast Keres, and Hopi is shown. Here is one more example of the outgrowth of a new pottery style from the combination of influences that seems always to occur as the result of the movement of restless peoples to new homes.

After the great Indian revolt of 1680, Isleta Pueblo principally manufactured polished red wares, again with a paste resembling that of Santa Ana and San Felipe. It has been many years since any of this traditional style was made. Isleta is also the home of a group of immigrants from Laguna Pueblo who in 1880 founded the satellite Isleta village of Oraibi. There the new settlers turned out for the railroad's tourist market small pottery pieces with rather attractive decoration in black and red on white. The opaque, milk-white slip, sometimes polished, joins with the rather soft, dusty paste to distinguish these Isleta-made vessels from those made at Laguna. In recent years this style has been replaced by a somewhat more commercial product.

Sandia Pueblo has had no known ceramic tradition during the Historic period.

117
Jemez Black-on-white Ceremonial Bowl
Before 1700. Diam. 26 cm. Museum of New
Mexico, Santa Fe, N.M., cat. no. 19975

Since about 1700, Jemez Pueblo has produced
no traditional decorated pottery. Before then the
Jemez potters made an anachronistic style that
harks back to a time in the Prehistoric period in
which black-on-white pottery was widespread
among the Pueblo Indians. This sacred ceremonial bowl shows well the nature of the Jemez
style. Painted birds and sculptured frogs join with
some uniquely Jemez geometric figures to present a selection of their religious iconography.
The sculptured frogs resemble those of Zuni, as
in color plate XXX.

118
Gobernador Polychrome Jar
Circa 1750. H. 26 cm. Coll. Mr. and Mrs.
John Hopkins

Many mingled cultures produced this jar of Gobernador Polychrome. Following the bloody Spanish reconquest of the Pueblo Indians in 1694,
many Indians deserted their villages and joined
their former enemies, the Navajo, in the remote
Gobernador Canyon in Northwestern New Mexico.
These refugees brought pottery with them from
their home villages, and from the surviving examples of these vessels it can be ascertained that
the population consisted mainly of Tewa, Zia,
Jemez, Zuni, and Hopi. From this mixture, Gobernador Polychrome evolved. Here are combined
the body shape of Hawikuh Polychrome, the
rim flare of Tewa Polychrome, the red banding
on the underbody of the Rio Grande villages,
the yellow-pink favored by the Hopi Indians, and
decoration influenced by Jemez.

Acoma and Laguna Pueblos

Acoma and Laguna (early period)

Prior to 1700 Acoma Pueblo was noted for its magnificent glazed ware with convex jar bases. After the Pueblo Indian revolt of 1680, this pueblo turned from the creation of magnificent glaze wares to matte-paint wares, and the concave base became a standard feature for Acoma water jars. It should be noted that Acoma potters have traditionally tempered their clay with finely crushed sherds of pottery, so that nearly every broken vessel is saved for re-use in this manner. This is a distinctive feature of Acoma, Laguna, and Zuni pottery, affording a strong contrast with wares from the other pueblos. The vessels made today by Acoma potters may well contain fragments of Prehistoric glaze ware, some of them occurring for perhaps the second or third time in an Acoma vessel.

Ako Polychrome is the name given to the first matte-paint Acoma and Laguna vessels of the early eighteenth century (see color pls. XIX and XX; figs. 120 and 121). Jars of this type are uniquely sculptured. The underbody is tall and narrow, while the upperbody is swollen into a bulbous spheroid perched on the top. The effect is that of a giant mushroom. The opening is simply a hole with a slight thickening around it; there is no neck. Ako Polychrome decoration is painted on the swollen upperbody only, the underbody being all-over red. Red banding of the underbody is absent at Acoma, differentiating the vessels from those of the Rio Grande area. Both artistry and precision are excellent. The motifs used in the decoration show great preoccupation with the feather symbol, reflecting a strong trend of the period. About 1730 Ako Polychrome rim tops changed in color from red to black.

About 1770 necks were added to the jars. The neck was only a short upward projection, several centimeters above the upperbody, at first not decorated but subsequently embellished with simple geometric motifs such as arcs and scallops. The resulting pottery type is called Acomita Polychrome (see color pls. XXI–XXIII; figs. 122–126). Towards the end of the eighteenth century the simple addition of a neck was joined by several others features. In particular, these Acomita Polychrome vessels are usually characterized by thicker, heavier walls, and considerably greater boldness in decoration. Two varieties can be recognized: the earlier has little or no neck decoration, but what there is, is especially striking — bold, black, and strong; the later has more elaborate neck decoration, which incorporates red.

In summary, Acomita Polychrome differs from Ako Polychrome in the following ways:

1 Addition of a neck.
2 Shortening of the underbody.
3 Less differentiation between the underbody and the swollen upperbody.
4 Thicker lines in the decoration than previously, with motifs that are larger and less formal in their arrangement.
5 Sloppier workmanship, resulting in less perfect form, thicker walls, poorer quality of slip.

Acomita Polychrome motifs are attractive in their simplicity and boldness. They incorporate the abundant use of the spiral volute, usually with little more than one turn because of the thickness of line. Massive red areas also are commonly used, often incorporating within their boundaries unpainted negative areas in crescent or semicircular form. There is a resemblance to early Santa Ana Polychrome, and sometimes the only sure way to differentiate them is to examine the paste closely. Santa Ana vessels have orange-tan clay with abundant fine, river-worn sand, unlike Acomita Polychrome's gray or tan clay with crushed sherds.

Acoma Pueblo

Through a gradual transition accomplished by about 1850 the Acoma vessels became a type that is now known as McCartys Polychrome (see figs. 127–130 and 132). (McCartys and Acomita are names of Acoma farming villages.) McCartys Polychrome resumed the well-executed, handsome decoration of the Ako Polychrome tradition but with an entirely new set of motifs. McCartys Polychrome vessels have several distinguishing features:

1   The jars are no longer sculptured into a lower and an upper body. The surface of one part simply curves smoothly to that of the other. The neck is no longer abruptly differentiated.
2   Once again the walls of the vessels are usually relatively thin, light, and strong.
3   The paste is almost always a clear white color. The slip, too, is whiter than previously.
4   The decoration begins to incorporate birds and floral motifs. They are relatively free and informal and more careful in execution.

In this period, also, there was considerable diffusion of decorative styles among the various pueblos. Similar parrot motifs coexist at Zia, Acoma, and Laguna, and even spread to Santo Domingo as late as the early twentieth century. Zuni Pueblo shares certain scroll-type motifs with Acoma Pueblo. It should be mentioned again that red banding of the underbody is absent from all vessels from Acoma and Laguna.

Around the turn of the century the last of the Acoma Pottery styles, Acoma Polychrome, evolved (see color pl. XXIV; figs. 131–135), with water jars predominating. In form Acoma Polychrome jars have several new features:

1 The neck shortens — becomes more a simple incurving of the upperbody to the opening.
2 Reflecting the trend of the time, the greatest diameter is placed distinctly higher than mid-height, resulting in a prominent shoulder just below the strongly incurving upper slopes.
3 The underbody, differentiated only by the boundary between the red and the white slipped areas, is much shorter than before.

Another modification characterizing Acoma Polychrome is a myriad of new motifs executed in a crowded morass of geometric patterns. Actually, many of these design components are revivals of long-neglected Acoma Pueblo motifs, some dating to Prehistoric times. A most remarkable panorama of swirls, circles, zigzags, and other abstractions is present. Although busy, the finest of the designs are delicate, complex, and creative, making effective use of reds and oranges. Usually the vessels are strong, well formed, carefully decorated, finished, and fired, demonstrating the traditionally high standards set by Acoma potters. Especially notable are the light, thin walls of Acoma water jars, a technical feat unrivaled by the rest of the pueblos. Serviceability has been as prominent a requirement of Acoma water jars as beauty. This also extends to bowls, although it should be noted that few Historic Acoma bowls have been preserved. Until recently the jars have been excellent water carriers. In all, Acoma vessels have continued to be among the finest made, although a recent unfortunate trend has been to incorporate into the clay materials that expand after firing, resulting in numerous pits or flecks that mar the surface. This same difficulty has also occurred occasionally at Zia Pueblo.

It should be mentioned that only a very few examples of ceremonial vessels from Acoma and Laguna are known. On rare examples of seemingly secular vessels from both Acoma and Zia may be found small dabs of greenish pigment applied after the pottery had been made. There is some evidence that these vessels have been used in the sacred Indian ceremonies.

Laguna Pueblo

Laguna, founded about 1700, followed so closely the Acoma pottery tradition that vessels made prior to about 1830 are difficult to ascribe to the correct village. Acomita Polychrome is a type common to both pueblos. But while McCartys Polychrome was evolving at Acoma, the Laguna wares were turning into Laguna Polychrome (1830–1930; see color pl. XXV; figs. 136–140). Laguna Polychrome jars retain more of the Acomita Polychrome traits than do the contemporary jars from Acoma. The distinguishing features of Laguna Polychrome of this period are:

1   A slight angular flexure is present, especially on the earlier vessels, where the outflaring (and sometimes slightly concave) lower body meets the convexly rounded upper slopes.
2   Stone-polishing stroke marks are often visible on the white slip.
3   The walls of the vessels may be heavier.
4   The paste contains crushed sherds and, often, much sand or many dark fragments.
5   Red is more lavishly used on interiors of bowls and as broad stripes in interiors of jars.
6   Often bands of interconnecting motifs in red encircle a vessel. Frequently they are bolder and less intricate than the more conservative motifs on Acoma Polychrome. Laguna also produced sculptured wares in interesting forms in which animals predominate.

After about 1900 Laguna pottery production began to decline, and since about 1920 the output has been almost neglible. The imprint left by Laguna Polychrome at its colorful zenith in the late nineteenth century is, however, impressive and important, as demonstrated by the large Stevenson collections in the United States National Museum.

119
Hawikuh Polychrome Jar

Circa 1680. H. 28 cm. School of American Research, Santa Fe, N.M., cat. no. 7832/12

This superb Acoma vessel is the only example of glaze ware illustrated in our book. Hawikuh Polychrome lasted until about 1700 among the Pueblos, being subsequently replaced by matte-paint pottery. The shiny mineral glaze, creating a vitreous surface, was admired chiefly for its beauty; overall glazing to waterproof pottery was never practiced. The technical and artistic achievements demonstrated in this Acoma vessel were never equaled in the cruder Rio Grande Pueblo glaze wares. Distinctive traits are the slight flexures of the body, the red slip covering the area below the top of the midbody, and the light buckskin tan slip bearing black-edged red motifs above the midbody.

120
Ako Polychrome Jars

Circa 1730. H. 25 cm. and 29 cm., respectively.
School of American Research, Santa Fe, N.M.,
cat. nos. 2999/12 and 3482/12, respectively

These early matte-paint jars, which succeeded
Hawikuh Polychrome from Acoma (see fig. 119),
are distinguished by having a concave base to
facilitate carrying the vessels on the head and a
decided flexure at the top of the underbody, forming a mushroom-like shape. Earlier traditions
retained are the slight lip and the all-red underbody. Typical split-feather and key-symbol motifs
of the early eighteenth century predominate in
the decoration. The bird beak on the jar at the
left leads into tail feathers and to some extent

shows Hopi Indian influence. A red rim top on
this vessel indicates a date prior to about 1730,
while the black rim top on the right-hand jar may
indicate a slightly later date.

121
Ako Polychrome Bowl

Circa 1720. Diam. 40 cm. Coll. Francis Harlow

The crosswinds of styles from San Pablo, Ashiwi,
and Puname Polychrome can be seen on this
typical Ako Polychrome bowl. Feather symbols
and key motifs compose the decoration. The entire underbody and the flat rim top are slipped
red and well polished. Notice the ceremonial
break at the center of the design.

122
Acomita Polychrome (Laguna Variety) Jar
Circa 1770. H. 28 cm. School of American Research, Santa Fe, N.M., cat. no. 7753/12

A rather short, undecorated neck and strong flexure below the midbody characterize this early Acomita Polychrome jar. The only red in the decoration occurs in the band at the base of the neck. In strong, bold design are an early version of the capped spiral volute and a coarse version of the feather symbol at the far left. The white-bordered rectangle is like those from Zia in figures 96 and 102. Compared to the best Ako Polychrome jars, this Acomita Polychrome vessel is much heavier and its walls are thicker, traits which, together with the strong flexure of the underbody, suggest origin at Laguna.

123
Acomita Polychrome Jar
Circa 1800. H. 28 cm. School of American Research, Santa Fe, N.M., cat. no. 2645/12

Although the neck is still short and undecorated, this Acomita Polychrome jar has distinctly evolved from the jar in figure 122. This is shown by the loss of flexure below the midbody, by the new form of the spiral volutes (drawn in wide red bands), and by the unpainted areas that have been left in both the red and the black motifs. These negative elements are traits that Zia shared briefly with Acoma and Laguna and that Santa Ana incorporated for many decades. Acomita Polychrome decoration tends towards informality and simplification compared to that of Ako Polychrome.

124

**Acomita Polychrome
(Laguna Variety) Jar**

Circa 1800. H. 27 cm. School of American
Research, Santa Fe, N.M., cat. no. 3483/12

Laguna may be the pueblo where this hand-
somely embellished Acomita Polychrome jar originated. Double or multiple dabs like those within
the ovals occur frequently on Acoma and Laguna pottery throughout the nineteenth century
(as, e.g., in figs. 125 and 126).

125

Acomita Polychrome Jar

Circa 1820. H. 25 cm. School of American
Research, Santa Fe, N.M., cat. no. 7833/12

This jar combines the earliness of a high, flexured
underbody with the lateness of a relatively tall,
decorated neck. The midbody decoration helps
resolve the paradox, showing in its arcs and rows
of dots a style that becomes especially common
after 1850.

126
Acomita Polychrome Dough Bowl

Circa 1800. Diam. 46 cm. Museum of New Mexico, Santa Fe, N.M., cat. no. 35763/12

Exuberant in pattern, this large dough bowl must have been an eye-dazzler when new. Unpainted arcs show the style popular at Acoma and Laguna around 1800 (see also fig. 123). In construction, the bowl is heavy and slightly askew in form. As on all Acoma–Laguna pottery after about 1740, the rim top is black.

127
McCartys Polychrome Jar

Circa 1870. H. 25 cm. Museum of New Mexico, Santa Fe, N.M., cat. no. 19082/12

The relatively high underbody and low placement of the maximum diameter combine with decorative style to identify this vessel as a jar of McCartys Polychrome. As at Zia (see fig. 110), foliage patterns (here split leaves) become common after about 1850, and interconnected oval designs are common in the latter half of the nineteenth century. A relatively tall neck is typical of McCartys Polychrome, but less so in the succeeding Acoma Polychrome.

XVII
Ranchitos Polychrome Canteen
Circa 1800. H. 39 cm. School of American
Research, Santa Fe, N.M., cat. no. 12519/12

This interesting canteen of Ranchitos Polychrome
shows the classic triangular-capped split-feather
symbol in a form embellished by the little spiral-
tipped crooks that became enormously popular
at Zuni nearly a century later (as, e.g., in fig.
152). Also evident are the triangular-capped
spiral volutes typical of Santa Ana and Zia pottery in the period 1780–1840. Except for the
clearly characteristic Santa Ana paste, this canteen might have been made at Zia.

XVIII
Santa Ana Polychrome Water Jar
Circa 1830. H. 27 cm. Coll. Francis Harlow

The most typical expression of Santa Ana Polychrome is exemplified by this water jar. Key
characteristics are the tan slip color, the red
decoration partly edged in black, the black rim
top, the absence of uppermost framing lines,
and the red-banded underbody. Most essential
is the orange-tan paste containing abundant
water-smoothed grains of light-colored sand,
which is a telltale sign of Santa Ana origin.

XIX
Ako Polychrome Jar
Circa 1700. H. 29 cm. School of American
Research, Santa Fe, N.M., cat. no. 3032/11

Made at Acoma just after the last Hawikuh Polychrome glaze ware was fired, here is Historic
Pueblo pottery at its most magnificent. Features
characteristic of Ako Polychrome are the concave base, tall proportions, matte paint, and
split feathers in a variety of forms. The rim top
is red, conforming to the Acoma style before
about 1740, and the underbody is all red,
in contrast to the red-banded style current
farther east. The rich orange-tan upperbody slip
is unusual.

XX
Ako Polychrome Jar
Circa 1750. H. 27 cm. Coll. Francis Harlow

A later version of the jar style shown in color plate XIX, this vessel has a strong and informal design of much visual power. The black rim top and slightly raised lip indicate the later date of manufacture. The checkerboard decoration occurs on both Acoma and Zuni pottery just prior to 1750 (as, e.g., in figs. 144 and 146). The upper-body walls are thin and light, while the under-body is heavy, a characteristic of several Ako Polychrome jars.

XXI
Acomita Polychrome Jar

Circa 1760. H. 25 cm. School of American
Research, Santa Fe, N.M., cat. no. 3009/12

The earliest stage of Acomita Polychrome, represented here, is distinguished by a short, undecorated neck and retains much of the form of
the preceding Ako Polychrome jars. The very
dark underbody and the use of two colors in the
decoration are unusual. The vessel walls are
relatively thick and heavy even in the upperbody. The rim top is red—an anachronism in
regard to Acoma, where black rim tops prevailed
by 1760. These attributes suggest that the jar
originated at neighboring Laguna.

XXII
Acomita Polychrome Jar

Circa 1770. H. 23 cm. School of American Research, Santa Fe, N.M., cat. no 2797/12

That this superb Acomita Polychrome jar is of the Laguna variety is indicated by the unslipped underbody, with heavy stroke marks from the polishing stone, and the unusual red banding, which may occur rarely at Laguna but probably never at Acoma. The bird motif resembles a similar one on Trios Polychrome (in fig. 100).

XXIII
Acomita Polychrome Jar

Circa 1800. H. 36 cm. School of American Research, Santa Fe, N.M., cat. no. 3036/12

This jar is typical of the Acoma variety of Acomita Polychrome, lacking the underbody sculpture that persisted for nearly a century longer at Laguna. The well-developed neck now receives a simple decoration, and the main field of the design has massive red areas with unpainted ovals and scallops, showing ties to Santa Ana pottery.

XXIV
Acoma Polychrome Jar
Circa 1900. H. 25 cm. Coll. Mr. and Mrs.
Larry Frank

Residual traits from McCartys Polychrome are
visible in the relatively low placement of the
maximum diameter and the two-band arrangement of the decoration of this colorful jar. The
vertical zigzag motif is an Acoma trait of the
period. The motifs of the pumpkin and corn-
fields (repeated on the other side) are unusual.

XXV
Laguna Polychrome Water Jar
Circa 1880. H. 24 cm. Museum of New Mexico,
Santa Fe, N.M., cat. no. 18704/12

The slightly concave underbody profile, the
stroke-marked slip, the relatively heavy weight,
the connected hearts motif, and the slightly
sloppy execution of the decoration distinguish
this very typical Laguna Polychrome water jar
from contemporary Acoma Polychrome jars.
Two colors appear in the decoration, an occurrence possibly more common at Laguna than
at Acoma.

Ashiwi Polychrome Jar

Circa 1720. H. 23 cm. School of American
Research, Santa Fe, N.M., cat. no. 2001/12

Baroque exuberance is exhibited in Pueblo pottery by this excellent, typical jar of Ashiwi Polychrome. Feather motifs, both capless and with
triangular caps, occur in the upper band of
decoration. The mythical bird figure has been
seen both on Puname Polychrome (as, e.g., in
color pl. XII) and on Hopi pottery of the period.
The rim top is red (as on all Zuni pottery before
1760) and the underbody is solid red, a feature
which persists at Zuni until about 1800. Figures
141 and 143 show motifs similar to those on
this jar.

Ashiwi Polychrome Jar

1710–1770. H. 22 cm. School of American Research, Santa Fe, N.M., cat. no. 2684/12

In form this jar is like that of Hawikuh Polychrome glaze ware, exemplified in figure 119, differing principally in the matte paint and concave base, but the black rim top here suggests a later date than the form does. Unusual features of the jar are the use of orange-tan, as in the jar in color plate XIX, and the contradiction of the crudely executed underbody and the finely executed upperbody, which indicates the vessel was made by two different artists.

XXVIII
Kiapkwa Polychrome Bowl
Circa 1750. Diam. 25 cm. University of Colorado
Museum, Boulder, Colo., cat. no. 395

A very early date for a Kiapkwa Polychrome
bowl is suggested by the red rim top, by the
simplified style of the decoration, and by the
discovery of the vessel shown here in a Gobernador Canyon refugee site dating no later than
about 1750. Features in contrast to those of
Ashiwi Polychrome are the unsculptured form
and the relatively low and dark underbody. The
exuberance of Ashiwi Polychrome is retained
here.

XXIX
Zuni Polychrome Water Jar
Circa 1880. H. 26 cm. Coll. Mr. and Mrs.
Larry Frank

The "dagger" motif on the neck band, the rosette
and birds, and the heartline deer motif all indicate clearly Zuni Pueblo. A pair of hooked
feathers forms each deer house. The heartline
deer motif, although traditional at Zuni, has been
found on pottery from Hopi and Acoma (as, e.g.,
in fig. 131). The meaning of the heartline motif
is unknown, but it has been incorporated into
sky serpents as well as deer.

XXX
Zuni Polychrome Ceremonial Jar
Circa 1890. H. 24 cm. Coll. Mr. and Mrs.
Larry Frank

The sculptured frogs and the large insect designs
(perhaps butterflies) are sacred figures that often
occur on Zuni ceremonial vessels. Such pottery
was used in supplications for rain, and Zuni
Pueblo is noted for having a host of mythical
water creatures: frogs, polywogs, water serpents,
dragonflies, and so on. The geometric figures
around the bottom and top of the midbody are
much like those on the underbodies of earlier
Zuni jars (as, e.g., in color pl. XXVII).

XXXI
Payupki Polychrome Bowl
Circa 1720. Diam. 11 cm. Coll. Francis Harlow

Typically Hopi in materials of manufacture, this
rare little bowl has in its decoration eastern
Pueblo motifs in almost all respects. The feather
motif is similar to that in color plate XIX. A very
similar treatment may be seen in the Ashiwi
Polychrome bowl in figure 144.

XXXII
Polacca Polychrome Jar
1800–1850. H. 27 cm. Coll. Mr. and Mrs.
Larry Frank

Especially characteristic of this magnificent jar
are the luminous yellow and orange hues used
on Hopi pottery since about 1300. The red rim
top, the red underbody, and the thick, finely
crazed slip covering the exterior are features of
Polacca Polychrome. The flower is typically
Hopi, resembling those in figure 165.

128
McCartys Polychrome Water Jar
Circa 1870. H. 25 cm. Museum of New Mexico, Santa Fe, N.M., cat. no. 1207/12

Simplicity in form and design are thoroughly typical of McCartys Polychrome, as in this water jar. A separate band of decoration on the neck is also quite characteristic. As in figures 127 and 129, there is an interconnection of the massive black-edged red elements, whose corners touch. The split leaves illustrate the popularity of foliage motifs.

129
McCartys Polychrome Jar
Circa 1880. H. 24 cm. Museum of New Mexico, Santa Fe, N.M., cat. no. 12031/12

The peculiar motif in the ovals of this jar is identical to the one on the jar from Zia in figure 108. The interconnected ovals with continuous red flowing between them are common for Laguna, Acoma, and Zia from 1850 to 1890. The checkered framing line in figure 128 is here expanded to commanding prominence. The tall neck and low position of the maximum diameter are characteristic features of McCartys Polychrome.

130
McCartys Polychrome Water Jar
Circa 1890. H. 25 cm. Museum of New Mexico, Santa Fe, N.M., cat. no. 12042/12

The much-evolved shape of this water jar shows that the vessel should be considered transitional to Acoma Polychrome. In arrangement the decoration resembles that of the Zia Polychrome jar in figure 107. Here, the two colored bands are of different hues, one being reddish orange and the other yellowish orange, making the vessel a true tetrachrome. The split-leaf foliage conforms to the repertory of ornament of the period, and the double dabs on the crest of the "eyed" triangles hark back to the earlier style of Acomita Polychrome, as in figure 126.

131
Acoma Polychrome Jar

Circa 1890. H. 48 cm. Museum of New Mexico, Santa Fe, N.M., cat. no. 12068/12

As in figure 130, the high shoulder on this jar suggests the period of transition from McCartys Polychrome to Acoma Polychrome. Reminiscent of typical McCartys Polychrome are the tall neck and the separate band of decoration around it. In style the decoration, however, shows the jar to be an early example of Acoma Polychrome. The deer figure exhibits the "heartline" from mouth to heart, a motif borrowed from Zuni. Zuni influence can also be seen in the hatched and solid interlocking spiral volutes.

132
McCartys Polychrome and Acoma Polychrome Jars

Left: Circa 1870. H. 26 cm. *Right:* Circa 1930. H. 29 cm. Museum of New Mexico, Santa Fe, N.M., cat. nos. 45792/12 and 12070/12, respectively

The McCartys Polychrome jar on the left and the Acoma Polychrome jar on the right contrast sharply in form and ornament. Note especially the tall neck on the splendid McCartys Polychrome jar, which has two shades of color in the diamond-shaped motifs, red on the outside and yellow-orange on the inside. The Acoma Polychrome jar has no color in the decoration.

133

133

134

134

133
Acoma Polychrome Bowls
Circa 1900. Diam. 30 cm. and 25 cm., respectively.
Coll. Mr. and Mrs. Larry Frank

Acoma Polychrome bowls seem to be less abundant than jars. The vertical hatched zigzag on the
typical jar to the right coincidentally resembles
the decorative band on the upperbody seen so
frequently on upper Rio Grande vessels of the
period 1760–1830, as in figures 64 and 65. Its
appearance on Acoma pottery appears limited to
a brief period around 1900. Neither bowl is decorated on the interior.

134
Acoma Polychrome Jars
Left: Circa 1900. H. 28 cm. *Right:* Circa 1920.
H. 26 cm. Coll. Francis Harlow

The hatched zigzag motif of the Acoma Polychrome jar on the left is the same as that in figure 133. The central diamond-shaped region has
a feather-like symbol in each corner. The jar on
the right is dominated by an example of the famous Acoma parrot. Parrots actually occurred in
the wild near Acoma until as late as 1880, and
have been revered as endowed with special abil-
ities to communicate with the gods. Outside the
oval the checkerboard pattern predominates in a
form that has been used at Acoma since as early
as 1750 (as, e.g., in color pl. XX).

135
Acoma Polychrome Water Jar
Circa 1910. H. 27 cm. Coll. Mr. and Mrs. Larry Frank

This Acoma water jar with borrowed Zuni motifs shows several characteristics of acculturation. The neck decorations, rim, heartline deer motif, and row of red birds are all features particular to Zuni. The medallion is an Acoma interpretation of the Zuni rosette motif (as, e.g., in fig. 154). In general, the Acoma handling of Zuni motifs tends towards the elaborate and baroque.

136
Laguna Polychrome Water Jar
Circa 1850. H. 30 cm. Coll. Mr. and Mrs. Larry Frank

This heavy little water jar of Laguna Polychrome has remained serviceable through many years of hard use. It shows a very early form of the flowers and foliage that dominate Acoma, Laguna, and Zia pottery in the last half of the nineteenth century. The tan, concave underbody, to which slip may not have been applied, presents an appearance typical of the earliest vessels that can be recognized as from Laguna (as, e.g., in fig. 124).

137
Laguna Polychrome Jars
Circa 1890. H. 29 cm. and 26 cm., respectively. Museum of New Mexico, Santa Fe, N.M., cat. nos. 12016/12 and 18705/12, respectively

These typical Laguna Polychrome jars are characterized by a slight angular flexure at the top of the underbody, a relatively low position for the maximum diameter, crudely stone-polished slip, relatively heavy weight, some crudity in the execution of the decoration, and a style of embellishment suggesting simplified McCartys Polychrome. The double dab motif can be seen on both water jars, while the one on the right has rows of dots somewhat like those seen in figure 125. Feather symbols dominate the neck-band decoration on the right-hand jar.

138
Laguna Polychrome Jar

Circa 1910. H. 26 cm. Museum of New Mexico, Santa Fe, N.M., cat. no. 18717/12

The concave slopes of the underbody of this Laguna Polychrome jar are a holdover from Ako Polychrome days, which persisted longer at Laguna than at Acoma. A low position for the maximum diameter is quite characteristic of Laguna Polychrome, as is the slip, which has more of a stone-stroked appearance than Acoma slip. Here is the ultimate in interconnection of the red motifs. Oblique rectangles like those in the upper band have been a persistent Pueblo Indian decorative device for many centuries. The heart-like motifs appear to have been an innovation of Laguna Pueblo.

139
Laguna Polychrome Bowl
Circa 1880. Diam. 21 cm. Coll. Mr. and Mrs.
Larry Frank

The decoration on this crude little bowl is similar to the traditional motif used in the upper
band in figure 138. Whereas red pigment appears
on the jar, an orangy yellow is applied to the
bowl, all the elements being interconnected in
typical fashion for the period.

140
Laguna Polychrome Ceremonial Bowl
Circa 1880. Diam. 21 cm. Coll. Francis Harlow

Like the underbodies of the jars in figures 124
and 136, the exterior of this very rare sacred ceremonial bowl is a stone-stroked tannish color
that is characteristic of Laguna. The slip on the
bowl's interior shows stone-stroke polishing
marks, also a Laguna trait. At its extremities the
"Maltese Cross" motif bears amazing heads of
mythological beings. Mythical animals (or insects)
attach themselves to corners of the cross. Hardly
any ceremonial vessels from Acoma and Laguna
are known.

Zuni Area

Zuni Pueblo

The early history of Zuni pottery is somewhat like that of Acoma and Laguna. All three villages traditionally use crushed potsherds to temper the clay. The Zuni paste differs in usually being a little coarser, having more pink chunks in it and, after 1850, being a little grayer in color. Moreover, when the surface erodes from an old Zuni vessel, the flake carries off some of the paste, while at Acoma the erosion more often means peeling of the curled slip only. After an earlier glaze-ware tradition like that of Hawikuh Polychrome (see fig. 119) at Acoma Pueblo in the beginning of the eighteenth century, Zuni Pueblo switched to mineral matte paint for decoration. The new matte-paint style is known as Ashiwi Polychrome (1700–1760), a type that at its best equals in magnificence any of the pottery of its time (see color pls. XXVI and XXVII; figs. 141–145). For a while the vessels from Acoma of that period also went by this name, but more recently some differences have been noted, leading to the name Ako Polychrome (see above, Acoma and Laguna Pueblos). Characteristics of Ashiwi Polychrome are as follows:

1 The jars are usually more squat than those of Ako Polychrome, with a widely flaring underbody, a midbody bulge, and gently inward-sloping upperbody.

2 This sculptural division into two regions above the underbody results in the use of two encircling bands of decoration, a simpler one of geometric motifs around the bulge, and a wider band of more complex motifs around the upperbody. Ashiwi Polychrome jars resemble in form and decoration the Puname Polychrome jars from Zia, but differ in paste and lack the red banding and red arcs of Zia.

3 As with early Ako Polychrome, the rim top and underbody of Ashiwi Polychrome are always red, the transition to black rim tops occurring about 1750 or a little later. Feather motifs predominate on vessels of Ashiwi Polychrome and are incorporated into elaborate and com-

plex patterns utilizing a variety of hooks, steps, and other embellishments. Bowls usually are simply jars minus the tall upperbody; the decoration often is relatively simple and geometric on the exterior and more complex and varied on the interior.

Kiapkwa Polychrome, named after the Zuni farming village, Kiapkwainakwin, is the next of the Zuni types (see color pl. XXVIII; figs. 146–151). Made in the period 1760–1850, this type sometimes shows a degeneracy similar to that of contemporary Acomita Polychrome vessels. In jars the greatest change of Kiapkwa Polychrome from Ashiwi Polychrome is the tremendous enlargement of the midbody, pushing the underbody into a low, flaring, inconspicuous section and squeezing the upperbody into a relatively short neck. On the neck the decoration is simple and formal, while on the central body region it is more elaborate, a trait that persisted thereafter at Zuni. Kiapkwa Polychrome jars show a decided flexure at the junction between lower body and middle body. This comes from the formation of the lower body in a pot-base mold, with the clay bulging over the edge at the top of the mold. On the early Kiapkwa Polychrome jars the underbody is polished red, but by about 1800 the style changed and underbodies were painted black, completely unique to Pueblo pottery. From then on, this unusual trait of black underbodies on both bowls and jars has persisted at Zuni with only rare exceptions. Early vessels of Kiapkwa Polychrome are beautifully and carefully decorated, whereas later ones are often rather sloppy.

At Zuni Pueblo there was a rare style of pottery, Zuni White-on-red, that perhaps survived as a holdover from Prehistoric days, in which the entire surface of the vessel was slipped a reddish color and decorated with motifs in white paint. Surviving examples seem to extend from about 1800 to perhaps as late as 1900.

Zuni Polychrome is the next and last of this succession (see color pls. XXIX and XXX; figs. 152–156). Emerging about 1850 this handsome type differs from its ancestor in the nature of the decoration and in the tendency to have the greatest width of jars placed somewhat above mid-height. The motifs of Zuni Polychrome are executed with elegance and precision, with much restraint exercised in the use of red. The only detraction is the persistent repetition of some of the more popular patterns; certain ones recur with almost no variation on hundreds of vessels. Common motifs are sunflowers, deer with a red arrow from mouth to heart (known as the heartline), tiny birds, butterflies, volutes (as on Trios Polychrome at Zia), modified hooked-feather symbols, and dagger-like figures. Interestingly, the Hopi and Acoma pueblos have occasionally borrowed the heartline motif from Zuni. The exterior decoration of bowls is conservative, almost none showing appreciable variation from a standard pattern of feather symbols on descending diagonals. Interiors of bowls were more freely decorated in patterns resembling those of the exteriors of jars. Especially attractive are the creamy white slip and the jar form.

The relative geographic isolation of Zuni Pueblo has led to the development of a distinctive style for sacred creatures on ceremonial vessels. Many of these are associated with water. The water serpent has a heartline from mouth to heart, a traditional Zuni attribute. Frogs, tadpoles, and dragonflies are abundantly represented on the sacred vessels. A common Zuni fashion is the terraced-rimmed prayer meal bowl, often with handles. In another type of ceremonial vessel, unique to Zuni, secular vessels are adapted for ritual use by drilling a hole in the side and several smaller holes around the rim to permit the tying on of carved antler fetishes. Such vessels are occasionally covered with finely crushed turquoise and shell; many recent imitations have come on the market. Some Zuni ceremonial jars have sculptured frogs on the sides.

As at Laguna, the potter's craft at Zuni has gradually faded away. The last fine vessels were made in the early 1900s. Subsequent vessels were made purely for sale as works of art and are cool-fired, therefore soft and porous, and do not hold water.

141

141
Ashiwi Polychrome Jar

Circa 1720. H. 23 cm. Museum of New Mexico, Santa Fe, N.M., cat. no. 7878/12

Ashiwi Polychrome, derived from the earlier Hawikuh Polychrome (see fig. 119), was manufactured at Zuni. The sculptural features are a flaring underbody, a midbody bulge, and a converging upperbody. There is no real neck. In form and in arrangement of the motifs Ashiwi Polychrome has a greater similarity to Puname Polychrome (as, e.g., in fig. 93), manufactured at Zia, than to Ako Polychrome (as, e.g., in fig. 120), manufactured at Acoma in the same period. Like Puname Polychrome and Sakona Polychrome (for the latter, see fig. 5), the midbody bulge has a narrow band of decoration while the upperbody has a wide band. The stepped triangles on the right are capped with little "three finger" devices, which recur in countless variations throughout the Historic period; an inverted example is seen in figure 142. When the jar is compared to the bowl in figure 143, it can be seen that if the upperbody had not been built the jar would have been a typical Ashiwi Polychrome bowl. The underbody is polished red, a color which persisted at Zuni until 1800, and the rim top is red, a trait that was followed at Zuni until about 1760.

142
Ashiwi Polychrome Jar

Circa 1730. H. 24 cm. Coll. Francis Harlow

A slightly taller underbody and lack of the typical feather symbols of the day distinguish this jar from the one in figure 141. Note, at left, the ceremonial break of the lines encircling the rim.

142

143
Ashiwi Polychrome Bowl

Circa 1730. 33x35 cm. School of American Research, Santa Fe, N.M., cat. no. 2017/12

Omission of the upperbody from a jar like that in figure 141 results precisely in the bowl form illustrated. Many motifs from the decoration of that jar and the one in figure 142 occur here, including the classical triangular-capped, split feathers, key motifs, stepped spirals, and hooks. Red slip covers the undecorated areas on the interior of the bowl.

144
Ashiwi Polychrome Bowl

Circa 1740. Diam. 27 cm. University of Colorado Museum, Boulder, Colo., cat. no. 394

This Ashiwi Polychrome bowl is from a refugee site at Gobernador Canyon. The rim top is red. A checkerboard at the center and numerous key motifs and variations of the feather symbol compose the decoration. The whole creates an effect of overwhelming visual delight.

145
Ashiwi Polychrome Bowl

Circa 1740. Diam. 40 cm. University of Colorado Museum, Boulder, Colo., cat. no. 396

A lip of the kind usually placed at the rim of a jar has been built inside the rim of this Ashiwi Polychrome bowl, found at a refugee site in Gobernador Canyon. The rim top and the entire underbody are painted red. In the decoration are double-ended key motifs somewhat similar to those on the Ako Polychrome bowl in figure 121.

146
Kiapkwa Polychrome Bowl

Circa 1750. Diam. 25 cm. University of Colorado Museum, Boulder, Colo., cat. no. 397

An early example of Kiapkwa Polychrome from Zuni Pueblo, this bowl is similar in decoration to the jar in figure 147. On the exterior to the right are checkerboard motifs like the one in figure 144, and in general there is a close relationship between early Kiapkwa Polychrome and late Ashiwi Polychrome. Red is used here for the underbody and rim top, as on all other vessels from Zuni dating before about 1760.

147
Kiapkwa Polychrome Jar

Circa 1750. H. 24 cm. University of Colorado Museum, Boulder, Colo., cat. no. 410

In comparison with Ashiwi Polychrome, the crucial features for Kiapkwa Polychrome jars are the enormous enlargement of the midbody and the reduction of the upper body to a short neck encircled with relatively simple motifs. Although such traditional features as feather symbols are clearly present on this jar, the decorative style heralds new patterns that would occur abundantly at Zuni more than a century later (as, e.g., in figs. 154 and 155). Only on this example of the earliest stage of Kiapkwa Polychrome are both the underbody and the rim top red. After about 1760, the rim top is black, while the red underbody persisted until about 1800.

148
Kiapkwa Polychrome Bowl and Jar
Left: Circa 1800. Diam. 30 cm. *Right:* Circa 1770.
H. 25 cm. Coll. Francis Harlow

The excellently painted jar on the right still shows
the relatively high, bright red underbody derived
from Ashiwi Polychrome. The decoration of the
midbody is based on key motifs. A concavity and
an angular flexure occur at the top of the underbody. By this time, the rim tops of jars have
been changed to black. Triangular-capped feathers decorate the exterior of the black-rimmed
bowl on the left, heralding the style of figure 153.

149
Kiapkwa Polychrome Jar
Circa 1820. H. 33 cm. School of American Re-
search, Santa Fe, N.M., cat. no. 7717/12

Many changes in the form and style of decoration
seen here have evolved from the jar in figure 148.
In form, the underbody retains the concavity
and the flexure at the top, exhibited by the older

jar. The neck, sharply differentiated from the midbody, is crested by a small lip at the rim, a feature that persisted longer at Zuni (until about 1900) than elsewhere. In the four-panel arrangement, two wide and two narrow, of the decoration of the neck the influence of San Pablo Polychrome can be seen. Triangular-capped spiral volutes and circles dominate the decoration of the midbody. Many of the motifs used, including the stylized birds, occur in modified form on later Zuni and Zia jars (as in figs. 154, 98, and 103, respectively).

150
Kiapkwa Polychrome Water Jar
Circa 1840. H. 23 cm. Coll. Francis Harlow

The later period of Kiapkwa Polychrome shows a marked degeneracy, as is indicated by this little water jar. The midbody decoration, consisting of interlocking solid and hatched key motifs, occurs with considerable frequency at Zuni during the first half of the nineteenth century. In form, the concave underslopes with flexure at the top are still present in incipient form, and the jar has a low placement of the maximum diameter. The neck is crested by a slight lip.

151
Kiapkwa Polychrome Jar
Circa 1850. H. 20 cm. Coll. Mr. and Mrs. Larry Frank

Like the jar in figure 150, this degenerate jar hovers in time between the great period of Kiapkwa Polychrome in the past and the magnificent flowering of Zuni Polychrome to come in the nineteenth century. Above the usual concave underslopes with cresting flexure is a midbody with the Kiapkwa Polychrome profile on the right but a high shoulder in Zuni Polychrome style on the left. There is no sharp differentiation of the neck and no lip. The ceremonial break in the upper framing line is dramatically apparent.

152
Zuni Polychrome Jar

Circa 1880. H. 31 cm. School of American Research, Santa Fe, N.M., cat. no. 2782/12

Here is Zuni Polychrome in its most exuberant profusion of precisely executed decoration, typical of the period. Every available area has been filled with spiral-tipped crooks. Arrangement of the decoration in two wide panels and two narrow panels still occurs at this stage. The heartline deer motif is evident, as well as a decorative band showing several figures of does.

153
Zuni Polychrome Bowl

Circa 1880. Diam. 35 cm. Museum of New Mexico, Santa Fe, N.M., cat. no. 16156/12

The red underbody of this bowl demonstrates the rare persistence of this eighteenth-century trait until as late as 1880. The exterior decoration, derived from a combination of the descending feathers in figure 148 and the red feather filling in figure 141, occurs with almost unrelenting monotony on bowls of Zuni Polychrome. The interior decoration is predominantly formed of the spiral-tipped crook figures seen in figure 152, but the delicacy there is here replaced by boldness.

154
Zuni Polychrome Jar
Circa 1880. H. 26 cm. Coll. Francis Harlow

Constructed with thin, hard walls and deftly painted, this jar testifies to the final Zuni ceramic florescence. It is traditional in form and in arrangement of the decoration. The large rosette on the left is a uniquely Zuni adaptation of the motif. Typical features of Zuni Polychrome decoration are the "dagger" symbols at the left of the neck band and, on the midbody, the little red birds with crook tails and the hooked feathers adjacent to the spiral volutes.

153

154

155
Zuni Polychrome Jar

Circa 1890. H. 25 cm. Coll. Francis Harlow

The meandering hatched key motifs on this jar are similar to those on the jar in figure 148, an earlier and more precisely painted version. The later jar is basically traditional in form, but the little red triangles dangling from the shoulder framing line and the dots alternating with hatched areas in the band on the upperbody become especially common in the late period here exemplified. The central motif of the decoration has been called the "Rainbird" by H. P. Mera.

156
Zuni Polychrome Canteen

1850–1900. H. 25 cm. Coll. Mr. and Mrs. Larry Frank

Similar canteens were produced at Zia, Acoma, Zuni, and the Hopi pueblos for several centuries. The form is derived from Prehistoric canteens on which the handles, like those on little ceremonial jars, were attached horizontally, rather than vertically as in this example. Traditionally, the narrow mouth was closed with a corncob to prevent spillage or evaporation of the water inside. The decoration on this canteen is a crude version of the rosette motif seen in figure 154, suggesting that the vessel was made somewhat near the end of the classic Zuni Polychrome period or possibly during the degenerate stages of Kiapkwa Polychrome.

Hopi Area (Arizona)

The Hopi Villages

In a remote section of northeastern Arizona, far removed from the rest of the Pueblo world, there are seven ancient villages and several modern ones occupied by the Hopi Indians and by Pueblo immigrants from the Rio Grande area. For over six hundred years Hopi pottery has been distinguished by its beautiful shades of yellow mottled with orange and by the fact that on most types the motifs are painted directly on the polished paste rather than on a slip. Another important feature is that unlike the other Pueblo Indians the Hopi almost never made vessels with concave bases, their vessels usually having flat or convex bases.

Historic Hopi pottery inherited an extremely rich tradition. In late Prehistoric times, just before the arrival of Europeans, the Hopi made some of the most magnificent vessels of the Pueblo world. In the seventeenth century, however, the production of these famous Sikyatki Polychrome vessels ceased, and excellence gave way to considerable decadence. San Bernardo Polychrome vessels from this later period are heavy, poorly constructed, and sloppily painted (see fig. 157). These crude, unslipped vessels are decorated with a mineral paint and often incorporate red in the motifs and on the rim tops.

About 1700 a new influence from the east arrived in the Hopi area, brought by refugees from several Rio Grande pueblos who fled from their revolt-torn land and established the Hopi towns of Hano and Payupki. The resulting new pottery type is known as Payupki Polychrome (see color pl. XXXI; fig. 158). This differs from earlier types in sometimes having a thinly slipped surface and a new style of decoration emphasizing the eighteenth-century feather symbol. The next Hopi type, Polacca Polychrome, was made in the period from somewhat before 1800 until about 1900 (see color pl. XXXII; figs. 160–164). The rim tops and underbodies of the vessels are usually red, but the most characteristic feature of this type is the thick, crackled slip applied before the decorations were painted. One form of Polacca Polychrome vessel is especially distinctive, the "mutton-stew" bowls with widely flaring sides. During the 1880s, a time concurrent with the Zuni ceramic revival, many of these Polacca Polychrome bowls were decorated in delicate figures somewhat like the Zuni fashion. The results, elaborate in design, are tasteful and beautiful in a baroque way. Lacy little loose-spiraled figures predominate, in combination with enough traditional Hopi motifs to give a local flavor.

There is a pottery type, Polacca Black-on-yellow (see fig. 159), which is an occasional variant of Polacca Polychrome. It occurs whenever red has been omitted from the design.

At the same time that the Polacca Polychrome thick-slip ware was being produced, the no-slip tradition continued. On Walpi Polychrome, dating approximately from 1750 to the present, no slip is applied on the smooth yellow-to-orange surface (fig. 165). These vessels were most often made in the form of jars. Commonly they were decorated with handsome and relatively realistic bird and floral motifs, especially after 1850, often absorbing motifs from other pueblos. The decorations were conceived with pleasing simplicity and restraint. As the nineteenth century drew to a close, Hopi ceramic output was declining in quantity, and the art might have nearly died out had it not been for a fortuitous event. At that time, excavations were being made at the Prehistoric village of Sikyatki, and among the onlookers was one particularly gifted artisan, Nampeyo of Hano Pueblo. When Nampeyo saw some of the beautiful pottery fragments found by the diggers she became determined to revive the ancient Sikyatki Polychrome style. This she accomplished with great skill and artistry, using her own versions of the old designs on no-slip pottery that was executed with nearly the same degree of excellence as that of the ancestors of her Hopi neighbors. The results were sensational; a whole new school of Hopi pottery arose, created by Nampeyo (who died in 1942) and her talented family. This style dates from just before 1900 to the present. Nampeyo found an eager market for her wares, and this stimulated other potters from the Hopi villages to produce similar vessels. Hano Polychrome (see fig. 166), Nampeyo's new pottery style, is produced simultaneously with Walpi Polychrome, and it is principally by the design that one is able to distinguish the two. Walpi Polychrome motifs of birds and flowers are more realistic and identifiable and sometimes primitive, while Hano Polychrome motifs copy the Prehistoric Sikyatki patterns that are usually more abstract and sophisticated.

By these and the following means Hano Polychrome can be distinguished from the ancient Sikyatki style:

1   Hano Polychrome vessels have a softer, more dusty-looking paste.
2   The black paint of Hano Polychrome is less permanent, smudging when rubbed vigorously with a damp finger.
3   Hano Polychrome decoration is usually more fussy and intricate, adding some modern motifs unknown to the ancient Sikyatki potters.
4   There are slight differences in the form of vessels.

In addition to the principal Hopi types discussed in this book, there are various others that have arisen in the last eighty years. For example, one may occasionally encounter vessels with a smooth red slip and decoration in black and white. Another even rarer recent type has a beautiful pure white slip on which the decoration has been painted.

157

157
San Bernardo Polychrome? (Ceremonial) Vessel and Bowl

17th Century? *Left:* H. 12 cm. Coll. Mr. and Mrs. Larry Frank. *Right:* Diam. 23 cm. Museum of New Mexico, Santa Fe, N.M., cat. no. 45231/12

158

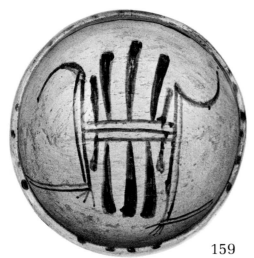

159

The earliest Hopi Indian pottery of the Historic period is represented by the bowl on the right and possibly by the exotic little (ceremonial?) vessel on the left. San Bernardo Polychrome is a highly degenerate version of Sikyatki Polychrome of the Prehistoric period. No slip covers the well-smoothed paste on which the decoration in black and red was painted in mineral pigments. Heavy walls, lopsided forms, and sloppy execution of the decoration characterize this type.

158
Payupki Polychrome Bowl

Circa 1740. Diam. 26 cm. University of Colorado Museum, Boulder, Colo., cat. no. 158

A strong eastern Pueblo influence, especially in the feather symbols, has been combined here with some distinctly Hopi innovations to produce this bowl characteristic of Payupki Polychrome. Typical of this ware (see also color pl. XXXI) is the treatment of the feather tips, with one side angular and the other rounded. The rim top is reddish brown in color, while the exterior is an unslipped yellowish tan. Found at the Gobernador Canyon refuge site, this vessel exemplifies the Hopi contribution to the mingling of cultures that took place there.

159
Polacca Black-on-yellow Bowl

18th Century? Diam. 18 cm. Coll. Mr. and Mrs. Larry Frank

This fascinating bowl exhibits an enigmatic decorative style that sometimes occurs on Hopi

ceramics. Although simple and crude, there is an unmistakable charm here. Clearly seen is the crackled slip that characterizes Polacca Polychrome, but no red is present in the decoration. Black dots encircle the rim.

160
Polacca Polychrome Jars

Left: Circa 1850. H. 21 cm. *Right:* 1750–1880. H. 25 cm. Museum of New Mexico, Santa Fe, N.M., cat. nos. 12080/12 and 11019/12, respectively

The spiral volutes on the jar to the right are bird beaks and the four long "fingers" between the volutes are tail feathers derived from an ancient Sikyatki motif, perhaps like those in figure 159. The hatched crescents are fairly common on Polacca Polychrome. As on much Hopi pottery, the red slip on the underbody is streaked and variable in thickness. In decoration the jar on the left was greatly influenced by the New Mexico pueblos, where a narrow ornamental band on the lowerbody was surmounted by a wider band on the upperbody, a style prevailing during the first half of the eighteenth century. The four-panel arrangement, with two narrow panels, and two wide, was inherited from Zia (San Pablo Polychrome) by way of Zuni (Kiapkwa Polychrome). Present also is the triangular-capped volute in the fashion highly typical of early nineteenth-century New Mexico pueblo pottery. Typical Hopi embellishments are seen, for example, in the hatched crescent leaves of the plant attached to the framing line.

161
Polacca Polychrome Bowl

Circa 1880. Diam. 30 cm. Coll. Francis Harlow

This "mutton stew" bowl with its considerable depth and widely flaring rim is a highly characteristic Hopi form. Crackled slip is a Polacca Polychrome feature. The red rim top suggests a date before 1880. In the decoration there are two opposing pairs of isolated motifs, the one on the far left being particularly common.

162
Polacca Polychrome Bowl

Circa 1820. Diam. 30 cm. Museum of New Mexico, Santa Fe, N.M., cat. no. 45232/12

This early bowl of Polacca Polychrome has features that relate in form and decoration to Kiapkwa Polychrome in about 1800 (as, e.g., in figs. 146 and 148). On the exterior the principal Zuni-Hopi feathers are placed on a diagonal. The red key-motif filling is somewhat like the version in Polacca Polychrome seen in figure 161.

163
Polacca Polychrome Jar

Circa 1880. H. 28 cm. Museum of New Mexico, Santa Fe, N.M., cat. no. 50000/12

Kachina faces with feather headdresses begin to appear on Hopi pottery about 1880. The ceremonial break in the framing line of the upper-body resembles that of the Zuni style at that date, also tending to confirm the age (see figs. 154 and 155). Between each pair of triangular-capped feathers is a thin-line triangle with double-ended crook like those in figure 161.

164
Polacca Polychrome Jar

Circa 1870. H. 18 cm. University of Colorado
Museum, Boulder, Colo., cat. no. 22/342

This jar is a typical Hopi form and a veritable
dictionary of Hopi decorative motifs. The third
band from the top has a variant of a motif that
has persisted for a millennium on Pueblo pottery;
see, for example, figure 5 and the Tewa Polychrome jar in color plate I. The hooked motifs in
the large midbody band suggest Hopi brocaded
sash designs. At the top of that band and in the
highest framing lines, ceremonial breaks can be
seen.

165
Walpi Polychrome Water Jar

Circa 1890. H. 26 cm. School of American
Research, Santa Fe, N.M., cat. no. 2397/12

Relative realism in the parrot figure characterizes this large Walpi Polychrome water jar. The
base of the jar is convex, a persistent feature of
most Hopi jars. Derived from San Bernardo Polychrome, Walpi Polychrome has motifs in black

and red mineral paint applied directly to the
well-polished paste, in contrast to the use of slip
in the Polacca Polychrome tradition. Stippled,
smudged-like fillings, as on the bird's body, are
unique to Hopi pottery. The characteristic Hopi
flower resembles the one on the Polacca Polychrome jar in color plate XXXII, and the arch
above the bird is related to Zia Pueblo styles, as
in figure 107 and color plate XVI. The subtrape-
zoidal form with short neck is typical of Hopi.

166
Hano Polychrome Jar

Circa 1900. H. 22 cm. Coll. Mr. and Mrs. Larry Frank

Like Walpi Polychrome, Hano Polychrome decoration is painted in black and red mineral pigments directly on the well-smoothed unslipped paste; however, it is the decoration itself, initiated by Nampeyo of Hano Pueblo shortly before 1900, that distinguishes Hano Polychrome. Nampeyo's motifs, adapted from Prehistoric Sikyatki Polychrome, are the comma-like spiral and the red-filled figure appended to its base. Notable Hopi traits are the convex base and, in color, the beautiful warm yellow that is a Hopi "trademark."

GLOSSARY

Aging – The continual changes effected by environment and time, producing an appearance that differs from the initial look of a newly fired vessel. Typical examples are cracking, abrading or rubbing, and the accumulation of natural oil that produces a beautiful polish or patina during years of handling.

Angular flexure – A sharp bend in the surface, sometimes occurring, for example, at the place where the erect rim of a bowl joins the underbody.

Arcs and scallops – Decorative features occurring in either the painted decoration or the sculpture of a vessel. A series of adjacent red-painted arcs, for example, is a common feature of Zia pottery in the early eighteenth century, while sculptured scallops on the rims of bowls and jars are often seen on the black pottery from Santa Clara, Pojoaque, and Nambe.

Ashiwi Pueblos – The Pueblo Indian villages in the vicinity of Zuni.

Band – An area of decoration encircling a vessel, usually bounded above and below by encircling framing lines and sometimes divided into rectangular panels.

Black-on-black – A technique of painted decoration in which dull mineral paint is applied to part of the polished red slip and the entire vessel turns black when fired in a smudging fire. The decoration thus shows as a textural contrast, not as a color contrast.

Bowls – Vessels with an opening at approximately the greatest width.

Buckskin color – The creamy tan color of a slip often seen on the early Historic pottery of Zia and Acoma; also occurring on hand-worn pottery from many of the other pueblos.

Canteen – A small vessel with a relatively narrow neck and a pair of handles.

Carbon paint – A pigment derived from vegetation, usually the Rocky Mountain bee plant or the tansy mustard. The juice from leaves and stems is concentrated into a watery brown liquid that soaks into the vessel and chars to a permanent black during firing. The soaked-in appearance, which allows the polish on the slip to show, contrasts with mineral paint, which covers the surface. Carbon paint on Historic pottery is characteristic of the Tewa and Northeast Keres pueblos (see map).

Ceramics – Pottery.

Ceremonial break – An interruption in any painted line encircling a vessel, or sometimes in a circular motif on a vessel. This commonly occurring feature is also called a "line break" or a "spirit path."

Ceremonial vessel – One that is used in the sacred rites of the Indians' religion. These vessels are usually painted with symbols related to Indian mythology and are sometimes sculptured with stairstep terracing along the rim.

Clay – The basic mineral substance from which pottery is manufactured, in combination with a tempering material and water.

Cochiti slip – A mineral substance, said to be predominantly bentonite, used to coat the surface of vessels at Cochiti and Santo Domingo pueblos, and after 1907 at San Ildefonso and sometimes Tesuque. Cochiti slip is usually polished with a rag and looks quite different from the stone-stroked local slip of the Tewa pueblos.

Combed – A textural feature of pottery, especially from Picuris, characterized by random groups of shallow parallel grooves.

Concave – Bulging inwards away from the viewer.

Convex – Bulging out towards the viewer.

Crackling – A synonym for crazing.

Crazing – Covered with small meandering cracks.

"Dagger" motif – A decorative feature of Zuni pottery, sometimes copied at Acoma and elsewhere, the appearance of which is that of a dagger or knife with stylized handle. The actual meaning of the motif, however, is probably unrelated to the name by which it is sometimes designated.

Design – The overall pattern of decoration, usually composed of motifs, which in turn are formed of various elements.

Dimpling – The effect produced when the polishing stone skips over the surface of a vessel, leaving a pattern of high points and depressions. This is especially characteristic of Tesuque pottery.

Dough bowl – A large bowl, usually used for mixing bread dough.

Effigy – A vessel formed into a human or animal shape, sometimes used for ceremonial purposes. Effigies are relatively rare in Pueblo Indian ceramics.

Element – A part of a motif, which if further subdivided would lose all distinctive meaning or appearance.

Ellipsoidal shape – Like a sphere that has been made taller or shorter rather than strictly spherical.

Fire clouds – Dark spots on the surface of a vessel, caused during firing by the smoldering of a piece of fuel against the surface.

Firing – The heating process by which the vessel is hardened. Pueblo Indians traditionally use no kiln, instead simply piling the fuel over the vessels and setting the whole on fire. Maximum attainable temperatures are accordingly low, no more than 950° C. At some pueblos recent pottery has been fired at even cooler temperatures in order to preserve luster at the sacrifice of strength. By comparison, commercial firing temperatures for pottery are 1200°–1400° C.

Flexure—Strong curvature—in some cases even angularity—of the surface of a vessel.

Floating—A polishing technique in which the unslipped clay is repeatedly stroked with a smooth stone in order to bring the finest-grained material to the surface, where it can be polished to a relatively high gloss.

Footed bowl—A bowl with an attached "ring" stand, or foot, that provides a support at the base. The foot is rarely prominent, usually being simply a thickening around the lower part of the underbody. Ceremonial bowls from Tesuque are often footed.

Framing line—A horizontal line, often occurring in pairs, encircling a vessel. Usually its purpose is to delineate a specific area or band of decoration.

Fuel—The material used in firing pottery, usually dried dung, bark, sticks, and sometimes coal (especially in the Hopi area).

Glaze—A material painted on the surface of a vessel, composed of minerals that melt during firing and then re-solidify to make a more or less glassy surface. Pueblo Indians have never glazed the entire surface of their vessels to waterproof them. Glaze paint was used principally in the period 1250–1700 but only as a pleasing complement to the decoration.

Guaco—The concentrated juice of the Rocky Mountain bee plant, used as a paint for pottery decoration.

Heartline motif—A motif, originating in the mid-nineteenth century, in which animal figures on pottery (especially deer) are depicted with a painted line from mouth to chest, terminating in an arrowhead at the position of the heart. Predominantly a Zuni decorative device, the heartline is also used at Acoma and the First-Mesa Hopi pueblos.

Historic—In the Pueblo Indian field, this term means dating after the arrival of the Europeans, effectively meaning after about 1600.

Incised—A technique of decoration in which patterns are scratched into the clay before a vessel is fired.

Invisible traits—These are such inconspicuous ceramics traits as material, tempering, strength of the vessel wall, and care exercised in polishing the interior of a jar.

Jars—Vessels, usually taller than bowls, with a much narrower opening than their greatest width.

Keel—A convex angular bend in the surface of a vessel, for example, the ones seen on the exterior of Tewa Polychrome bowls.

Key motif—Half of a rectangular figure with a stairstep diagonal. This figure is attached at one corner to a stem.

Kiln—An oven in which pottery is fired. The Pueblo Indians do not use a kiln in the ordinary sense, but instead form one with the fuel itself.

Line break—A short interruption in an encircling framing line, a common device that is also called a "ceremonial break" or "spirit path."

Lip—A slightly outflaring sculpture at the rim of a vessel.

Matte paint—A vegetal or mineral paint that does not melt during the firing of the vessel. Matte mineral paint is accordingly usually not shiny, while matte vegetal paint shows the surface finish of the adjacent unpainted slip.

Micaceous paste—A clay material that naturally embodies its own tempering of abundant mica flakes, used by the potters of Picuris and Taos. Nambe Polychrome is distinguished by the presence of large mica flakes in an otherwise typical Tewa paste, but this micaceousness is not nearly so apparent as in micaceous slip or a true micaceous paste.

Micaceous slip—A clay material that is especially rich in flakes of mica and that is painted on the surface of a vessel to give a metallic luster. Such vessels, usually made by Tewa potters, mimic the naturally micaceous ceramics of Picuris and Taos.

Mineral paint—A substance used in painting decoration on pottery. Three principal types can be distinguished: glaze paint, matte paint, and matte slip. Glaze paint is vitreous, matte paint is dull in finish, while both are usually shades of dark brown or black. Matte slips fire to red or orange or rarely to shades of pink, gray, or other hues.

Motif—One of a number of components of a scheme of decoration, arranged in a pattern; a dominant structure in an overall design.

Neck—The region, usually of a jar, adjacent to the opening and differentiated from the body by an area of curvature or flexure. Often the neck is more nearly vertical than the nearby walls of the body. Some jars, however, have no neck, the opening being simply a hole in the body. Some, for example, Ako Polychrome, have such a slight structure that it qualifies more properly as a lip than as a neck.

Negative—A motif, comparable to a negative photographic image, left unpainted in an otherwise painted surface.

Neolithic—The latest stage of human cultural development in which stone tools still predominate. The Neolithic period differs from earlier Stone Age periods in the gathering of habitations into villages, division of labor, practice of controlled agriculture, and usually the discovery of pottery making. The Pueblo Indians are an excellent example of Neolithic people, at a stage comparable to that of the Near East seven thousand years earlier.

Oxidizing fire—A pottery-hardening fire in which a sufficient draft of air is introduced to effect complete combustion. In Pueblo pottery the resulting colors are the warm shades of cream, tan, brown, red, orange, or yellow (compare Reducing fire).

Paint—A suspension of pigment used for decorating pottery. Examples are carbon paint, mineral paint, and glaze paint.

Panel—A rectangular area formed by means of vertical lines that divide a band in which decoration is placed.

Panel line—A vertical line, often occurring in pairs, separating two panels in an encircling band of decoration.

Paste—The mixture of clay and temper usually described in terms of its fired state.

Patina—Material gradually adhering to the surface of a vessel during use, after firing. The term is also applied to the general surface appearance as a result of aging. "Patina" is usually used in a positive or favorable sense, denoting pleasing consequences of aging, whereas "dirt" and "abrasion" often refer to the displeasing effect of aging.

Pitcher—A vessel with a handle on one side only; it may have a spout on the other side. Rectangular pitchers are used for ceremonial purposes at the Northeast Keres pueblos of Cochiti, Santo Domingo, and San Felipe.

Polishing—The process by which the surface of a vessel is smoothed before firing. Polishing may produce a gloss resembling glaze, or it may remove only the coarsest roughness. The two basic techniques are stone polishing and rag polishing. Stone polishing usually leaves stroke marks, which can vary from deep grooves to almost invisible traces. Rag polishing imparts a characteristic uniformity to the surface, which is usually finely striated from the structure of the fabric or leather rag and from the tiny grains of imperfection in the clay which may be dragged across the surface by the polishing cloth.

Polychrome—A decorative style utilizing more than two colors, for example, a white slip enhanced with black and red paints. Even if one of the additional colors is not part of the decorative field (for example, a red rim top on an otherwise black-on-tan bowl) the vessel is still classed as polychrome.

Positive—A motif rendered in paint (as opposed to one that is negative, left unpainted on an otherwise painted surface).

Pottery type—In classification, or taxonomy, all the vessels sufficiently similar to a designated standard constitute a type, identified by name. The type name has two parts; the first, a geographical name, is specific; the second, an attribute, is generic. Examples are Santa Fe Black-on-white and Tesuque Polychrome.

Prehistoric—Dating before the advent of a written history for the American Southwest, meaning prior to about 1600 for the Pueblo Indian world.

Prayer meal bowl—A ceremonial bowl, often with a

sculptured terrace along the rim, in which finely ground meal is placed. In certain prayers, a pinch of the meal is taken and symbolically sprinkled in the sacred directions.

Pottery—Artifacts of clay and other materials that have been hardened by firing.

Puddle—To bring water to a vessel's surface so that the surface can be floated (see Floating) and then polished.

Pueblo—Means village in Spanish; in the present context we refer to a village of the Pueblo Indians or, as a proper name, to this Indian people or their culture.

Puname area—The district in and around the present pueblos of Zia and Santa Ana.

Rag polishing—See Polishing.

Rawhide thongs—Such thongs were often used to bind together a vessel that was cracked. They are illustrated in this book on a storage jar of Powhoge Black-on-red.

Red—An earth color that actually can vary from dark brown through brick red and tan to light orange.

Red banding—A traditional embellishment of a vessel's underbody in which an encircling red band is painted just above the unslipped area and just below the white-slipped area of decoration. Red banding is a feature seen only on pottery from the pueblos near the Rio Grande, especially in the period 1650–1930.

Reducing fire—A pottery-hardening fire in which fresh air is excluded from the region where the pottery is baking. In Pueblo pottery the resulting color is a shade of gray-white, gray, or black (compare Oxidizing fire).

Revival—The re-occurrence of a trait or style that had previously been popular.

Rim—The part of the vessel immediately adjacent to the opening.

Ring tone—The sound emitted from a vessel whenever it is tapped. The tone varies from a clear, melodic bell-like ring to a dull thud. Cracked vessels may have a sharp but nonmusical sound. Clarity and duration of ring tone are not necessarily attributes of a fine vessel.

Scallops—See Arcs and scallops.

Sculpture—Usually refers to any departure of a vessel from the simplest utilitarian shape. But the term also refers to the relatively rarer formation of a ceramic artifact into a distinct representation of something other than a simple container.

Seepage—The transmission of liquid through the walls of a vessel. No newly fired Pueblo vessel is absolutely watertight (as a glazed jar would be) until the pores are sealed with fat or (alas) varnish. Cool-fired pottery, such as some of the modern black wares, are especially porous, and readily damaged by water. The more traditional wares, however, are completely serviceable for years without appreciable damage.

Sherd — A piece of broken pottery.

Shoulder — The region of a jar's greatest diameter, especially when this is relatively high.

Slip — A dilute mixture of fine red or white clay and water, mopped onto the surface of a vessel and then compacted and polished with a rag or stone. There are several purposes for slip: to cover the coarser paste, to make possible a smoother polishing of the surface, to make a better surface for painting and decoration, and to decrease seepage.

Smudging fire — This is a misnomer for a reducing fire, since the black is not simply a surface smudge of carbon but actually a permanent chemical change in the materials.

Stone polishing — The process by which the surface of a vessel is smoothed, floated, and polished by stroking it with a very smooth stone. The technique has long been used by many (but not all) of the Pueblo Indians. Well-worn stones are almost faceted from use by generations of potters.

Storage jar — A large pottery vessel, generally with a narrow opening, used especially for the storage of dry materials such as dried meat, grain, or vegetables. Storage jars are usually larger than about 30 centimeters in greatest dimension.

Taxonomy — The science of classification, referring here to the definition and naming of pottery types.

Temper — An inert material mixed with the basic clay and water to keep the substance from being too sticky and to reduce the likelihood of cracking during drying and firing. The kind of temper used traditionally at each village has been the same for centuries, and accordingly affords a means of identifying the place at which a vessel was manufactured. Examples of tempering materials are fine sand, powdered volcanic tuff, and crushed potsherds.

Terrace — A stairstep design, usually describing the sculpture along the rim of a bowl into an elevation, or a series of them, bounded on each side by stairsteps.

Type locality — A locality where examples of a particular type of pottery can be found.

Type name — The recognized name that designates all the examples of pottery that are sufficiently similar to a specified standard. The name consists of two parts; the first is geographical and the second is an attribute — for example, Cochiti Polychrome.

Type specimen — A specific vessel serving as a standard to which all other examples of a type can be compared.

Underbody — The part of the vessel lying below the area of decoration, or below the greatest width, or below the lowest flexure.

Upperbody — That part of the vessel lying above the middle body, if such can be clearly discerned, or else lying above the underbody, but in either case not including the neck.

Vegetal paint — See Carbon paint.

Volute — A spiral motif, in the Pueblo version usually having scarcely more than one turn.

Wall — The material part of a vessel, lying between the inside and the outside. In cross section the wall may have a central core, inner and outer parts, and perhaps an inner and/or outer layer of slip.

Water jar — A medium-sized vessel, from 20 to 30 centimeters tall, with a relatively narrow opening and often a concave base to facilitate carrying the vessel on the head.

BIBLIOGRAPHY

Bancroft, H. H. *History of Arizona and New Mexico, 1530–1888.* Albuquerque: Horn and Wallace, 1962.

Bunzel, Ruth. *The Pueblo Potter: A Study of Creative Imagination in Primitive Art.* New York: Columbia University Press, 1929. An early work by a noted anthropologist.

Bushnell, G. H. S., and Adrian Digby. *Ancient American Pottery.* New York: Pitman Publishing Co., n.d. A book specializing in Precolumbian pottery, with fine illustrations, some of Prehistoric wares from the region of Zuni.

Carlson, Roy L. *Eighteenth-Century Navajo Fortresses of the Gobernador District.* Series in Anthropology, no. 10. Boulder, Colorado: University of Colorado Press, 1965. Features Historic Pueblo pottery of the first half of the eighteenth century, with excellent illustrations and text.

Chapman, K. M. "Indian Pottery." Exposition of Indian Tribal Arts, Inc., *Introduction to American Indian Art,* Part II, pp. 3–11. New York, 1931. Articles by many experts on Indian art, with illustrations. Chapman's article is a brief introduction to the whole range of American Indian pottery, emphasizing Southwest Prehistoric and Historic ceramics. Well illustrated.

———. *Pueblo Indian Pottery.* 2 vols. Nice, France: Szwedzicki, 1933, 1936. Visually the most exquisite work on the subject; brief text. Illustrations focus on early Historic Pueblo pottery from the Indian Art Fund.

———. *The Pottery of Santo Domingo Pueblo.* Laboratory of Anthropology, Memoir I. Santa Fe, 1939. Styles of decoration are profusely illustrated. Brief account of the background of the pottery.

———— and B. T. Ellis. "The Line-Break, Probing Child of Pueblo Pottery." *El Palacio*, vol. 58 (1951), no. 9, p. 251. Focuses on charting pottery in relation to the line-break feature; has analysis of Historic pottery.

———— and F. H. Harlow. *The Pottery of San Ildefonso Pueblo*. Santa Fe: School of American Research, 1970. A tribute to Chapman, who died before he finished the book. It illustrates numerous motifs from San Ildefonso pottery, and the text treats the entire range of this pueblo's pottery production.

Christensen, E. O. *Primitive Art*. New York: Thomas Y. Crowell Co., 1955. A general survey with fine illustrations, including some of Pueblo pottery.

———— and L. L. Hargrave. *Handbook of Northern Arizona Pottery Wares*. Museum of Northern Arizona, Bulletin no. 11. Flagstaff, 1937. Good guidelines to determining pottery types; a functional, descriptive handbook of Northern Arizona Prehistoric pottery.

Colton, H. S. *Potsherds: An Introduction to the Study of Prehistoric Southwestern Ceramics and Their Use in Historic Reconstruction*. Museum of Northern Arizona, Bulletin no. 25. n.p., 1953. Indispensable to scholars. A clinical study of the entire field, with a thorough analysis of Prehistoric Pueblo pottery.

————. *Pottery Types of the Southwest*. Museum of Northern Arizona, Ceramic Series no. 3C. Flagstaff, 1956. Condensed but primary material on Hopi Historic pottery.

Covarrubias, Miguel. *The Eagle, the Jaguar, and the Serpent*, pp. 201–229. New York: Alfred A. Knopf, 1954. An important book on Indian Art of the Americas. Discusses Southwestern Prehistoric archaeology and, briefly, Historic pottery. Many drawings.

Dockstader, Frederick J. *Indian Art in America*, plates 153–157. Greenwich, Connecticut: New York Graphic Society, 1961. A lavish pictorial survey of American Indian art with a few illustrations of Historic Pueblo pottery.

Douglas, F. H. *Modern Pueblo Pottery Types*, pp. 53–54; Denver Art Museum Leaflets. n.p., 1933. Thumbnail sketch of pottery characteristics during 1930–1940, describing stylistic changes.

———— and Rene d'Harnoncourt. *Indian Art of the United States*, pp. 105–109. New York: The Museum of Modern Art, 1941. One of the first comprehensive surveys of Indian Art as a whole to be published in this country. There are brief references to Southwest pottery and some illustrations.

Dunn, Dorothy. *American Indian Painting of the Southwest and Plains Areas*, pp. 98–108. Albuquerque, University of New Mexico Press, 1968. A brief general summary of stylistic features of the pottery of

various is presented, with pueblos illustrations.

Dutton, Bertha P. *New Mexico Indians: Pocket Handbook*. Santa Fe: New Mexico Association on Indian Affairs, 1951. An account of the Pueblo Indians for the general public. Well illustrated.

Ellis, F. H., and J. J. Brody, "Ceramic Stratigraphy and Tribal History of Taos Pueblo." *American Antiquity*, vol. 29 (1964), no. 3, pp. 316–327. Covers the process of dating Taos Pueblo pottery.

Fewkes, J. W. "Archaeological Expedition to Arizona in 1895, Part II." *Seventeenth Annual Report of the Bureau of American Ethnology*, pp. 519–742. Washington, D.C., 1898. A classic work on Prehistoric Hopi pottery from 1400 to 1600, with beautiful color plates and comprehensive text.

Field, Clark. *Indian Pottery of the Southwest Post-Spanish Period*. Tulsa: Philbrook Art Center, 1960. Includes some illustrations of Historic Pueblo pottery with occasional incorrect identifications of the pueblo of origin.

Frank, Larry. "The Art of Ancient Indian Pottery." *Nimrod*, vol. 16, no. 23 (Summer 1972). Artistic and cultural features of Pueblo pottery are discussed.

Gladwin, H. S. *A History of the Ancient Southwest*. Portland, Maine: Bond Wheelright Co., 1957. A noted anthropologist's stimulating and controversial account of Prehistoric Indians; a good overview.

Guthe, Carl E. *Pueblo Pottery Making*. New Haven: Yale University Press, 1925. Pottery-making techniques as typified by San Ildefonso Pueblo are thoroughly investigated.

Harlow, Francis H. "Ceremonial Pottery of the Tewa Indians." *El Palacio*, vol. 72 (1965), no. 4, pp. 13–23. An article focusing on unique ceremonial vessels from Tesuque and San Ildefonso. Illustrated.

————. *Historic Pueblo Indian Pottery*. Santa Fe: Museum of New Mexico Press, 1967. The first recent attempt to reclassify Historic Pueblo pottery, this pamphlet accurately describes its range. Includes drawings.

————. *Matte Paint Pottery of the Tewa, Keres and Zuni Pueblos*. Museum of New Mexico Press, 1973. A detailed technical description of pottery in the period 1650–1920. Numerous halftones and drawings.

———— and John V. Young. *Contemporary Pueblo Indian Pottery*. Santa Fe, New Mexico: Museum of New Mexico Press, 1965. A pamphlet briefly classifying modern Pueblo pottery, with illustrations.

Hawley, Florence M. *Field Manual of Prehistoric Southwestern Pottery Types*. University of New Mexico Anthropological Series, vol. 1, no. 4. Albuquerque, 1936 (revised 1950). Describes briefly significant Prehistoric and early Historic Pueblo pottery.

Hewett, E. L., and B. F. Dutton. *Pojarito Plateau and Its Ancient People*. Albuquerque: University of New

Mexico Press, 1953. The ancestral place of origin of the Tewa Indians is described; also the use of potsherds to determine dates for the material culture.

Hodge, F. W. "Circular Kivas near Hawikuh, New Mexico." *Contributions of the Museum of the American Indian, Heye Foundation*, vol. VII, no. 1, New York, 1923. Early Zuni Historic pottery types are described.

Kidder, A.V. "Ruins of the Historic Period in the Upper San Juan Valley, New Mexico." *American Anthropologist*, vol. 22 (1920), no. 4, pp. 322–329. Deals with the Gobernador period of pottery in the early eighteenth century.

——— and C. A. Amsden. *The Pottery of Pecos, I: The Dull Paint Wares*. Papers of the Phillips Academy Southwestern Expedition, no. 5. New Haven, 1931. An invaluable illustrated reference work on early Historic Pueblo pottery, such as late Tewa styles, black on white, and polychrome of the early eighteenth century. A classic work.

——— and Anne O. Shepard. *The Pottery of Pecos, II: The Glaze Paint, Culinary and Other Wares*. Phillips Academy. New Haven: Yale University Press, 1936. Text and illustrations center on glazed pottery of the Pecos region and on an evaluation of Pecos wares in general. Key source on glaze ware.

Lambert, Marjorie F. *Pueblo Indian Pottery: Materials, Tools and Techniques*, Santa Fe: Museum of New Mexico Press, 1966. A reference work on pottery making.

O'Kane, W. C. *Sun in the Sky*. Norman: University of Oklahoma Press, 1970. Repr. of 1950 ed. The making of Hopi ceramics is mentioned.

Parsons, Elsie C. "Isleta, New Mexico." *Forty-seventh Annual Report of the Bureau of American Ethnology*. Washington, D.C., 1932. A short account of the way immigrants from Laguna Pueblo influenced Isleta pottery.

Shepard, Anne O. *Ceramics for the Archeologist*. Carnegie Institution Publication no. 609. Washington, D.C., 1956. A scholarly treatise on technical features.

Smith, Watson, R. B. Woodbury, and N. F. S. Woodbury. "The Excavation of Hawikuh." *Contributions of the Museum of the American Indian, Heye Foundation*, vol. 20. New York, 1966. Early types of Zuni pottery from region of Zuni are illustrated and analyzed.

Stevenson, James. "Illustrated Catalogue of the Collections Obtained from the Indians of New Mexico and Arizona in 1879." *Second Annual Report of the Bureau of [American] Ethnology*, pp. 307–422. Washington, D.C., 1880–1881. Also: "Illustrated Catalogue of the Collections Obtained from the Indians of New Mexico in 1880." Ibid., pp. 423–465. An account of Stevenson's foray into Zuni, Acoma, Laguna, and related pueblos in 1879 and 1880, and the illustrated report of the pottery collection he assembled for the Smithsonian Institution.

Stevenson, Matilda Coxe. "The Zuni Indians." *Twenty-third Annual Report of the Bureau of [American] Ethnology*, pp. 273–377. Washington, D.C., 1901–1902. One of the definitive works on the Zuni Indians, richly illustrated; Zuni pottery making briefly described, with a few illustrations.

Stubbs, Stanley A. *Bird's Eye View of the Pueblos*. Norman: University of Oklahoma Press, 1950. Interesting aerial photographic views and maps of the Southwest pueblos and their architectural complexes, with a short description of each pueblo.

——— and W. S. Stallings, Jr. *The Excavation of Pindi Pueblo, New Mexico*. School of American Research and Laboratory of Anthropology, Monograph 18. Santa Fe, 1953. Early black-on-white pottery from the Tewa region is thoroughly discussed.

Underhill, Ruth. *Pueblo Crafts*. [Indian Handcrafts no. 7.] Washington, D.C.: Bureau of Indian Affairs, 1944. A good book for the general public, showing ceramic techniques and illustrations of late classic Pueblo pottery.

Wedel, Waldo R. *Prehistoric Man on the Great Plains*. Norman: University of Oklahoma Press, 1961. With this book comparison can be made between Great Plains pottery and fifteenth-century incised ceramics of the Tewa region.

Wendorf, Fred. *Salvage Archeology in the Chama Valley, New Mexico*. School of American Research, Monograph 17. Santa Fe, 1953. Relationships among some early Tewa pottery types are brought out, based on excavation findings.

Wormington, H. M., and Arminta Neal. *The Story of Pueblo Pottery*. Denver: Denver Museum of Natural History, 1951. Good illustrations of a few examples of Prehistoric and modern pottery, with a succinct text on the distribution of styles.

GLASSBORO STATE COLLEGE